Preaching in a Tavern

and 129 other surprising stories from Brethren life

Kenneth I. Morse

Brethren Press®
Elgin, Illinois

Brethren Press® is a trademark of the Church of the Brethren General Board, 1451 Dundee Avenue, Elgin, IL 60120.

Illustrator: Jan Gleysteen

Brethren Press gratefully acknowledges The Brethren Encyclopedia, Inc., 313 Fairview Avenue, Ambler, Pennsylvania 19002-4307, for permission to reprint sidebar articles by Kenneth Morse from *The Brethren Encyclopedia* to form the core of this collection. Morse is inspired to publish these seventy- seven anecdotes and other stories from Brethren publications and his personal files in order to enliven history and promote interest in the church's past and its future.

01 00 99 98 97   5 4 3 2 1

Library of Congress Cataloging-in-Publication Data:

Morse, Kenneth, 1913-
Preaching in a tavern and 129 other surprising stories from Brethren life / Kenneth I. Morse.
p. cm.
Collection of articles from The Brethren encyclopedia and other stories from Brethren publications.
Includes bibliographical references and index.
ISBN 0-87178-005-4 (pbk.)
1. Church of The Brethren—History—Sources. 2. Church of the Brethren—Biography. I. Title.
BX7815.M67 1997
286'.5—dc21   96-51491

Manufactured in the United States of America

This book is affectionately dedicated to the memory of my grandparents John and Anna (Sowers) Bennett.

They were parents to six sons and six daughters and grandparents to thirty-five children. Grandfather, himself the oldest of eleven children, had so overworked his body that he developed a curvature of the spine, which could not be corrected. This did not result in a deformity of the spirit, however—in fact, quite the opposite. He took normal school courses provided by Bedford County to prepare himself for the thirteen winters he taught school. Add this to the daily running of the farm, so important for a growing family, and managing a community store. Grandfather was also the postmaster for thirty-three years at Artemas, Pennsylvania. From the postal station at the front of his house, this one rural community kept in touch with the larger world through its daily mail service.

More important to Grandfather than the community's relationship to the world, however, were the relationships of people in the church. For almost sixty years, he was a Brethren minister. He was baptized in 1874 in the Snake Spring congregation (which then included the Artemas area), called to the ministry in 1876 at a love feast in Israel Bennett's barn, and ordained an elder in 1897. Grandfather Bennett was instrumental in organizing the Glendale and Amaranth congregations, which he served as a free minister in addition to the church at Artemas. He represented his district on Standing Committee at three Annual Conferences, one at St. Joseph, Missouri, and two at Winona Lake, Indiana. Living in an isolated area where he was often the only resident minister, Grandfather provided pastoral services for hundreds of people who were not members of his church. Unfortunately, his active ministry was severely curtailed during the last ten years of his life because of blindness.

Not discouraged by his blindness, Grandfather seemed to walk in a light of his own. My favorite memories recall him in later years sitting on his porch swing or walking back and forth singing a song that the Brethren liked to sing. It included this lively refrain, which celebrates God's loving kindness.

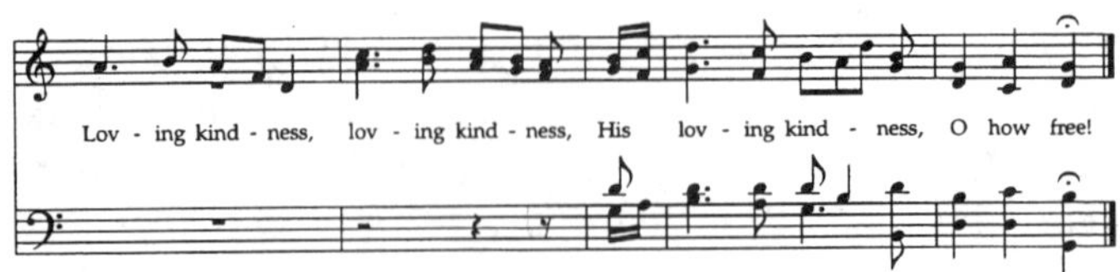

Contents

The Scrappers Get Together (peace and justice)

The Widow and the General (witness)

Sparks from the Hoff Anvil (Brethren personalities)

91. "The Touch of the Master's Hand"
92. Sparks from the Hoff Anvil
93. Raspberry Seeds: the Quotable William Beahm
94. "More Than You Promise"
95. Falling Among Thieves
96. Man of Many Gifts
97. Pole-Vaulting Preacher
98. A Fortissimo Man
99. Blindness No Handicap
100. An Episode in Modern Medical History
101. Inventive Genius
102. The Peace Connection
103. He Ate the Whole Thing
104. The Making of a Brumbaugh
105. A Man of Property and Principle
106. Life at Full Throttle
107. One of a Kind
108. In Search of Falling Stars
109. In the Front Seat with M. R. and Amy
110. The Teacher and His Teachings
111. The Alexander Mack Seal
112. Mack's Personal Bible
113. The Long and the Short

George Washington Came to Dinner (celebrity connections)

Preface

About thirty years ago, Reuel Pritchett said to me, "When we talk about *these things* I'm not eighty years old anymore. I can throw this cane out the window and keep up with the best of ye."

We were taking a roundabout way to our meeting in North Carolina, riding in Ron Wine's compact car—all three of us in the front seat. Ron was driving, I rode in the middle, and Reuel Pritchett, with his angular body, took his place next to the right door. This arrangement allowed Reuel to gesture outside and point to interesting sights as we rode through the beautiful mountainous area. I soon discovered that Brother Pritchett, who was thirty years older than I, would score a point in his conversation by coming down with the full strength of his left index finger onto my right knee.

"These things" of which Reuel spoke had to do with his early memories of Brethren meetings in eastern Tennessee and historic places still carrying Brethren names, such as Mack's Mountain and Max (Mack's) Meadow. He recalled festive occasions such as love feasts and Annual Meetings that he attended, personal accounts that were later published with the cooperation of Dale Aukerman in a book entitled *On the Ground Floor of Heaven*.

To talk about "these things" was rejuvenating for him. He no longer felt any constraint because of age as he shared with sheer joy his experiences of historical interest that have been collected in books, magazines, papers and even then were being placed in the Pritchett Museum at Bridgewater College.

Some years after that trip, I was on the editorial board of *The Brethren Encyclopedia,* which stimulated my interest in collecting stories and objects related to Brethren life. Many times as we considered topics to include in the encyclopedia, one of the board members would say, "That reminds me of a good story . . . ." This happened so frequently that the editorial board decided to include a number of such stories of Brethren life in the encyclopedia, set apart from the other material as sidebars. Since I was still in Elgin and had easy access to the Brethren Historical Library and Archives, the board asked me to prepare a number of these stories. Together with offerings from other contributors there must be more than a hundred sidebar stories in *The Brethren Encyclopedia.*

Now that I am the one who is over eighty and contending with walkers, canes, and a wheelchair, I can understand the frustration Brother Prtichett must have felt in becoming limited in his activity. But also now I can share in his enthusiasm for the church and all that it meant to him.

This book, which includes many of those *Brethren Encyclopedia* sidebars, is not offered as history. It is a collection of simple stories of people for whom loyalty to Christ and his church is effective for everyday living. It has been a spiritual experience for me to examine those stories, and I hope that you, as well, can respond to the humanness and humor of Brethren and the way they live from day to day. Hopefully, these values will be passed on to future generations through this collection.

Had I known two years ago the difficulties my health would cause, this undertaking would not have looked so inviting. But so many friends have offered encouragement during my struggle with Parkinson's disease and a hip replacement. Because my fingers are stiff, my typing has suffered, but our daughter Betsy has taken over much of that task. My wife, Marjorie, has exhibited *almost* unlimited patience, taking notes and searching for files and doing many other tasks.

I have much appreciation for Julie Garber, my editor, and her co-workers at Brethren Press, who have shown a great amount of patience with my slowing down and not always having stories sent on time. I am fortunate to be living at Timbercrest Church of the Brethren Home in a community where many people have been a part of these stories and where I have access to the Manchester College Archives, the well-supplied library at the Manchester Church of the Brethren, and the Manchester community library.

As I have become aware of certain disabilities, I have discovered the value of agencies that provide health care. I specifically want to acknowledge the Regency Health Care Center in Escondido, California, and the hospital there, and the special care I receive almost daily from Heartland Home Care. Wabash Hospital and Timbercrest Health Care have also been helpful with my recovery.

Kenneth I. Morse
North Manchester, Indiana
November 1996

Preaching in a Tavern

—worship

1

A Jubilee Journey

Celebrating fifty years in the ministry, I. N. H. Beahm undertook a two-hundred-mile journey during which he preached twenty times on twenty different topics at twenty locations—all in one day, July 26, 1931. He began what he called his "jubilee journey" at four A.M. at the C. W. Sutphin home in Fluvanna County, Virginia, where his sermon topic was "The Morning Star."

Beahm was accompanied on his journey by ministers who assisted in each service, singers from Reading, Pennsylvania, and three stenographers—he called them "recording angels"— who took down his sermons in shorthand.

As the day went on, Beahm preached in private homes, on church and court house lawns, and in several churches. He concluded with the twentieth sermon, on the subject "How to Be Saved and Church Ordinances," at Valley Church in Prince William County. At that evening service, Beahm said, "We have been practically on schedule all day long. I feel as I felt this morning, very weak, and yet I have felt the Lord to be with us today." He was seventy-two years old.

Beahm's sermons covered such topics as work, giving,

fasting, prayer, education, the state and the church as divine institutions, the positives and the negatives of Christianity, and the supremacy of the Bible and the church. Having little use for notes, he was scornful of preachers who read their manuscripts: "The Holy Spirit makes notes but needs no notes to preach by. Note that."

Nearly twenty years after that jubilee journey, Beahm attended a love feast at Jones Chapel in Virlina and was on his way to another appointment when death came to him at the age of ninety-one. Desiring "to die with his shoes on," he was always on the go, promoting a brand of Christianity that required an immense amount of footwork. As an educator, churchman, and itinerant evangelist, he must have worn out many pairs of shoes.

The Brethren Encyclopedia. Philadelphia, Pa., and Oak Brook, Ill.: The Brethren Encyclopedia, Inc., 1983-84: 1168 (sidebar). Expanded.

Based on information and manuscripts of the twenty sermons provided by Mary Beahm Baber, daughter of I. N. H. Beahm.

2

An Eccentric Preacher

Peter Lutz was known as an able but eccentric preacher. Both in western Pennsylvania and in Iowa, where he moved in 1844, he was accustomed to walking ten to fifteen miles to fill an appointment, often going barefoot on the way and standing thus in the pulpit. He quoted freely from the scriptures, and his sermons were considered unnecessarily long, even in that era.

At one time Lutz's closing prayer at a burial service lasted so long that everyone except one deacon left before he finished. When he spoke as a visiting minister at Communion services, other ministers would often pull his coattail to get him to sit down.

This unconventional style, along with his tendency to be outspoken, may explain why Peter Lutz, though considered a "power in the pulpit," was never ordained.

The Brethren Encyclopedia. Philadelphia, Pa., and Oak Brook, Ill.: The Brethren Encyclopedia, Inc., 1983-84: 1054 (sidebar).

Two Centuries of the Church of the Brethren in Western Pennsylvania, 1751-1950. Elgin, Ill.: Brethren Publishing House, 1953.

3

Preaching in a Tavern

George Price and several other Brethren ministers were visiting congregations in western Pennsylvania in the early 1800s. Seeking a night of rest, they found overnight lodging at a tavern, but the proprietor warned them that a dance scheduled for that night, predictably accompanied by loud music and boisterous behavior, might disturb them. Learning that the next inn was seven miles distant, the ministers decided to stay and "sleep through it."

When the leader of the dance expressed eagerness to meet the preachers and arranged for his friends to come along to meet with Price and his companions, the conversation proved so interesting that the dance was postponed and George Price was encouraged to preach to this impromptu congregation in the tavern.

J. E. Miller, who recounts the story, concludes, "Thus it came to pass that those who came to fiddle and dance heard a Dunker preach and pray."

The Brethren Encyclopedia. Philadelphia, Pa., and Oak Brook, Ill.: The Brethren Encyclopedia, Inc., 1983-84: 27 (sidebar).

Holsinger, H. R. *History of the Tunkers and the Brethren Church*, 1901.

Miller, J. E. *The Story of Our Church*. Elgin, Ill.: Brethren Publishing House, 1941, 1957.

4

The First Brethren Hymnal

The year is 1720. Two German composers, Johann Sebastian Bach and George Frederick Handel, are both in their prime at age thirty-five. Handel's career as a composer of operas has just been launched in England, where he has the favor of the king; and Bach, already recognized as an organist, is composing mostly instrumental music at a prince's court in Germany. It's a time, especially in Germany, when baroque music is flourishing.

Though a record company a few years ago published an album called *The Great Hits of 1720*, one will search in vain in that collection—or any other—for music from the first hymnal of the Brethren. Only in recent years have Brethren been aware of a remarkable hymn book, printed at Berleburg, near Schwarzenau, in 1720. It is a small book, attractively designed, containing German texts of hymns then being sung by separatist and pietist groups in Europe. It also contains a few hundred new hymns apparently written by Brethren. The title of the collection is *Geistreiches Gesang-Buch* . . . (Spiritual Songbook . . .).

The preface, as well as the character of several of the original hymns in the collection, provides valid reasons for regarding this book as the earliest Brethren hymnal. The preface explains that some worshipers did not like having to choose from many different hymnals: "For this reason we have been led to select the most edifying hymns from all of them and compile them in one volume."

The book contains hymns that celebrate such specific Brethren practices as the love feast and feetwashing. And the collection also includes a hymn by Alexander Mack, "Count Well the Cost."

It wasn't until the 1950s that Donald Durnbaugh, while searching in Europe for Brethren source materials, found a copy of the 1720 volume in the Wittgenstein collection in Marburg, Germany. Convinced that this rare book was indeed the first Brethren hymnal, he made copies of the hymns and translated the introduction into English; then he included it along with English translations of four of the hymns in his source book, *European Origins of the Brethren*, published in 1958.

To date only five copies of the 1720 hymnal are known to exist. Two of these had been kept at Marburg where they were the property of the state. As such, neither copy could be purchased, and Brethren had to be satisfied with occasional visits to the Marburg collection. Some years after Durnbaugh's discovery, an exchange of rare books was planned and effected in

February 1983 through negotiations with Dr. Martin Kraatz of Philipps University in Marburg, who was in charge of the Wittgenstein collection there.

Dr. Allen Deeter of Manchester College made the exchange during a visit to Marburg. He took with him two books, both published by Christopher Sauer in Germantown, that had been in the Brethren Historical Library and Archives in Elgin. These German publications of value to the Marburg collection were accepted in exchange for one of the two copies of *Geistreiches Gesang-Buch* . . . , which is now in the rare book collection of the Brethren Historical Library and Archives and has an honored place as one of the oldest Brethren publications.

The 1720 hymnal, printed only twelve years after the beginning of the Brethren movement at Schwarzenau, is tangible evidence of the importance of hymn writing and hymn singing among Brethren.

5
Sarah Major Kept On Preaching

James Quinter called her "a woman of energy and strong convictions . . . a remarkable woman," who overcame the obstacles to becoming the first woman preacher among the Brethren.

He was writing about Sarah Righter Major at the time of her death in 1884. By then she was well accepted in most churches, a very different situation than when, soon after her baptism in Philadelphia at age eighteen, she felt the call to preach. The minister of Sarah's church, Peter Keyser, encouraged her, but Annual Meeting would soon rule in 1834 that to allow women to preach "was not approved of." A year later Sarah wrote a long letter, later published, in which she defended the integrity of her call. She noted scriptural instances of women who were prophets. She even dared to take on the Apostle Paul, writing: "God always gave his gifts freely where they were willing to use them, and I believe in Christ Jesus male and female are one."

James Quinter also observed that, though Sarah had to contend with considerable prejudice in the brotherhood, once she was known she was loved for her modesty, her humility, her discretion, and her exemplary life. Wherever she went to preach, she was almost always invited to return.

Another contemporary described her preaching as "usually of the style of exhortation; but when treating some subjects, she spoke with great emphasis. She occasionally spoke on such subjects as infanticide and sexual excises [sic] in such a way as to make many blush, and some good brethren and sisters thought her words were sometimes imprudent."

Henry Holsinger had the experience of sharing the pulpit at the Philadelphia church with Sarah Major. He is perhaps a little more candid in confessing his own prejudices against women preachers and the importance of accepting the ministry of one so gifted as Sarah Major.

> Sister Righter had great influence over her audiences, and when she became deeply interested in her subject, she grew eloquent. Her appeals were especially effectual to those of her own sex.
>
> Notwithstanding the strong prejudice against women preaching, . . . Sister Righter's extreme modesty and her exemplary life subdued much of [the criticism], wherever she was once permitted to preach. I had the satisfaction of sharing the Philadelphia pulpit of the Tunker church sometime during the sixties of the nineteenth century with Sister Major. It was my turn to preach in the forenoon, and

> I confess I was guilty of a feeling closely akin to humiliation, at the thought of being in the same stand with a woman preacher. In the evening Sister Major preached, and I now humbly acknowledge that I was very much ashamed of myself and of my effort, but most of all I was dissatisfied with myself because of the prejudice confessed to above, but which I am thankful to have the assurance I had carefully concealed. She preached an excellent sermon. Her style was simple, her manner perfect, and every gesture in place.
>
> At the Sunday school, she was called on to address the children. The Sunday school was held in the gallery. Sister Major arose and walked around the pulpit-opening in the floor of the gallery, to a point opposite the writer. She stood for a moment, looking about as if to decide whether she was occupying the proper spot, when she said, "Years ago today, at this very hour of the day, I stood in this same spot; I was converted to Christ, and felt the assurance of my sins forgiven."

Sarah and Thomas Major were married March 10, 1842, by Elder Peter Keyser. Major was also a minister in the Brethren church. The couple raised three children, none of whom belonged to the Brethren fraternity.

Sarah Major's modest demeanor belied her daring not only to preach, but to speak out on controversial topics then seldom mentioned. She preached often in jails and hospitals. She and her husband were among the first to welcome black members and encourage them to become leaders in the church.

Durnbaugh, Donald F. "She Kept On Preaching." *Messenger,* April 1975: 18-21.
Holsinger, Henry. *History of the Tunkers and the Brethren Church,* 1901.

6

To His Name's Honor

Despite the opposition of many nineteenth-century Brethren to the ownership and use of musical instruments, Henry Kurtz kept in his possession and played in private a small pipe organ that he had brought with him from Germany in 1817. As recorder, compiler, and printer of Annual Meeting minutes, Kurtz was well aware that Brethren were advised not to use organs, even in their homes, unless they were "put way," which likely meant "kept out of public sight."

Henry R. Holsinger, who worked for Kurtz as an apprentice printer, said, "Brother Kurtz was quite a musician, vocal and instrumental. . . . I shall long remember one occasion on which I heard him perform and sing one of his favorites. . . . When I complimented him on his success, he explained that he had been tired of reading and writing, and had sought recreation and solace in the music." Kurtz's granddaughter later recalled visits to his room where the old organ stood in one corner. She said, "Sometimes he played on the organ and enjoyed teaching me some little songs on Sunday afternoons."

The organ was built in Nürttingen, Germany, in 1698 by John Christoph Harttman. The builder recorded the date and event in a barely legible inscription on the organ and included this prayer: "May God grant that many beautiful and spiritual psalms and songs may be played and struck in this work in His name's honor."

Harttman is known to have worked between 1682 and 1712 in the Württemberg region, and while his name is associated with several instruments, this organ is the only known extant example of his work, and it is also one of the oldest playable organs in the western hemisphere.

The organ was probably built for a resident of Tübingen, and it eventually became the property of Henry Kurtz, who may have brought it to the United States from his native Württemberg, as a twenty-one year old immigrant, in 1817. Kurtz, a Lutheran, was baptized into the Brethren church in Stark County, Ohio, in 1828, and soon became a well-known elder and minister.

C. C. Ellis saw and heard the organ in the home of F. J. Kurtz in 1898 and said, "Its music to us seemed scarce inferior to that of many modern instruments of greater pretensions." The organ was later dismantled and placed in a barn. The value of the decaying parts was realized by historian L. W. Schultz, and in 1957, L. P. Good, a great-grandson of Henry Kurtz, placed the organ in the care of the Brethren Historical Committee. Alvin F. Brightbill and Paul Bieber spent many hours salvaging the instrument, and in 1976 the General Board commissioned John Brombaugh & Co., of Middletown, Ohio, to restore the organ, an undertaking that took several men two full months.

The instrument has been on display at the Church of the Brethren Offices in Elgin, Illinois, since 1976.

The Brethren Encyclopedia. Philadelphia, Pa., and Oak Brook, Ill.: The Brethren Encyclopedia, Inc., 1983-84: 900 (sidebar). Expanded.

Durnbaugh, Donald F. "Standing Tall: The Life and Witness of Henry Kurtz." *Messenger*, April 1976: 13-16.

"To His Name's Honor." A pamphlet prepared at the time of the restoration of the Kurtz organ. Church of the Brethren General Board, 1976.

7

Music for the Everlasting Arms

Although most hymnals and songbooks credit A. J. Showalter for the music of "Leaning on the Everlasting Arms," Samuel Duncan, a member of the Oak Hill (Progressive) Brethren Church in West Virginia, claims that he wrote the tune when he was working as a young man with George B. Holsinger in the preparation of songbooks. The tune is one of the most popular of the thousands attributed to A. J. Showalter and has appeared in hundreds of songbooks.

Duncan said many years later, "I wrote just a plain, simple tune, and it happened to make a hit because it was wonderful words. When you have wonderful words, a plain tune is better. We didn't get it ready in time for our new book, but it soon found its way into other books. I do not know whether A. J. Showalter knew that I wrote the music. . . . We were busy getting the book published and didn't think or care about it."

Samuel Duncan taught singing schools and music classes in many communities, directed many church choirs, and managed a music store. He died in 1960.

The Brethren Encyclopedia. Philadelphia, Pa., and Oak Brook, Ill.: The Brethren Encyclopedia, Inc., 1983-84: 560 (sidebar).

Ankrum, Freeman. *Sidelights on Brethren History.* Elgin, Ill.: Brethren Press, 1962.

8

The Anxious-Bench Heresy

Christian H. Balsbaugh (1831–1909) minced no words when he denounced what he called "the anxious-bench heresy." In 1878 he wrote a short article for the *The Primitive Christian and Pilgrim*, entitled "In the Lap of Delilah," which aptly describes his feelings about a popular method of conversion.

> To make the anxious-bench anything else than a contemptible farce is to discount the Word and Work of God . . . . Ministering brethren who stimulate their lay members to attend anxious-bench revivals and assist by prayer and persuasion to decoy souls into this gospel-repudiating institution, are clear[ly] outside the function of a Heaven-appointed ambassador of the Cross. To coax the sin-burdened to come forward and kneel at the bench and wrestle in supplication until the Holy Ghost is bestowed, or sin remitted, is a gross violation of the order of God in Jesus Christ . . . .
>
> Away with this miserable, soul-cheating machinery for inducting sinners into the Divine favor. What was good enough for the Apostles, is good enough for us . . . . Conversion has no more to do with the anxious-bench than the doxology means the Yankee Doodle.

Balsbaugh continued the polemic by explaining that "regeneration means turning the soul Christward by the power of the Holy Ghost in the use of the Divinely-appointed means. Among these there is no anxious-bench, no infant-sprinkling, no homeopathic suppers at midday, no swindling of souls out of heaven by the trickeries of theological gamblers. 'I AM THE WAY, THE TRUTH, AND THE LIFE.' This will stand, whatever else will fall."

The Brethren Encyclopedia. Philadelphia, Pa., and Oak Brook, Ill.: The Brethren Encyclopedia, Inc., 1983-84: 930 (sidebar).

Balsbaugh, C. H. "In the Lap of Delilah." *The Primitive Christian and Pilgrim*, June 11, 1878.

9

A Son of Thunder

Known as the "Son of Thunder" because of his fearless and vigorous preaching, Samuel A. Fike (1820–1905) had a strong physique and rode many miles on horseback through the mountains of West Virginia to serve rural congregations.

Fike would take his coat off while preaching and lay it on a table before him. Once when he was reaching a dramatic climax in a sermon, he brought his fist down heavily on the table and smashed his watch to pieces. Yet his children said they never saw him angry.

The Brethren Encyclopedia. Philadelphia, Pa., and Oak Brook, Ill.: The Brethren Encyclopedia, Inc., 1983-84: 490 (sidebar).

Bittinger, Foster M. *A History of the Church of the Brethren in the First District of West Virginia*, 1945.

10

First Major Hymn Writer

Without any question the first Brethren hymn was "Count Well the Cost," written by Alexander Mack. And it appeared in the first Brethren hymnal, *Geistreiches Gesang-Buch* . . . . This hymnal, not discovered until the mid-1950s, was published in Berleburg in 1720. It contains 295 hymns, of which 101 were anonymous. According to the preface of the hymnal, other hymns were written by imprisoned Brethren, presumably the six Brethren men imprisoned at Solingen.

As one of the Solingen Brethren (six young men who were imprisoned from 1717 to 1720 at the fortress at Jülich), William Knepper, it is said, wrote more than four hundred hymns while imprisoned. After long and arduous work comparing the German text of the 1720 hymnal with two pietist hymnals that provided its non-Brethren material, Hedda Durnbaugh was able to identify which hymns were written by the imprisoned Brethren referred to in the preface to the hymnal. Her research concludes that it is likely that Knepper is the author of the one hundred anonymous hymns.

Knepper, a weaver, joined the Brethren in Solingen about 1716. Upon his release from prison in 1720, he joined the Brethren in Surhuisterveen, in northern Holland, where the Schwarzenau Brethren had gone to seek religious freedom. There in 1723 Knepper married a Mennonite, and in 1729 they sailed to America with a group under the leadership of Alexander Mack.

Today, along with "Count well the cost" (No. 437), one of Knepper's hymns—"How pleasant is it"—appears as No. 451 in *Hymnal: A Worship Book* (1992). It is a hymn of feetwashing, translated by Ora W. Garber. To be sure, William Knepper can be recognized as the first major hymn writer among the Brethren.

William Knepper's name is also associated with two devotional writings from the eighteenth century. One is an account, written by William Grahe, of the experiences of the six young men from Solingen during the years of their imprisonment at Düsseldorf and Jülich from 1717 to 1720. Although written about fifty years after that time, the story contains graphic details concerning the hardships and the courage of these men. The account was distributed widely in pietist circles, read in meetings, and copied frequently, serving as an inspiration to many. Donald Durnbaugh has included the text in his book *European Origins of the Brethren* (1958).

Just before his death, William Knepper composed the other devotional writing primarily for his family. It is a spiritual testament with reference to his beloved church and has been preserved by his family and printed in an English translation. The text of the 1880 edition appears in another Durnbaugh source book, *The Brethren in Colonial America* (1967).

Durnbaugh, Hedda. *The German Hymnody of the Brethren, 1720-1903*. Philadelphia, Pa., and Oak Brook, Ill.: The Brethren Encyclopedia, Inc., 1986.

Durnbaugh, Hedda. "*Geistreiches Gesang-Buch*, 1720: The First Brethren Hymnal." *The Hymn*, October 1991: 20-23.

11

A Ministering Sister

As a young girl, Laura (Grossnickle) Hedrick would spend time in her father's store, a community meeting-place in Mapleville, Maryland. One evening she quietly listened to local loafers and then recorded their conversations in shorthand. The next day, to their consternation, she gave them a verbatim report of their comments the evening before.

Laura's eagerness to spread the news was not satisfied with an airing of local gossip. Something of a pioneer (she began public school teaching at age seventeen), Laura was also interested in preaching the good news of the gospel. An organization of the Brethren Church known as the Sisters' Society of Christian Endeavor extended to her the call to preach and encouraged her to become a pioneer in an area where women were not welcome—as ordained ministers of the gospel. Henry Holsinger said of her, "So strongly did the need of earnest workers appeal to her heart that she offered herself to Christ to do whatsoever he would have her do. . . . [Her call] seemed to come directly in answer to prayer and she dared not refuse."

Despite the initial opposition to her ministry, Laura

Hedrick persisted until she was ordained in 1891 and continued to advocate a more active role for women in the ministry. She was one of several women who served as pastors and preachers in the Brethren Church in the 1890s and early 1900s. They were encouraged by policies adopted by the denomination's General Conference in 1892 and 1893 and by the editorial support of A. D. Gnagey, who wrote in the *The Brethren Evangelist* in 1895 that "women ministers are distinctly a product of the advanced period of the nineteenth century."

The Brethren Encyclopedia. Philadelphia, Pa., and Oak Brook, Ill.: The Brethren Encyclopedia, Inc., 1983-84: 1362 (sidebar).

Ankrum, Freeman. "Laura Grossnickle Hedrick." *The Brethren Evangelist*, Feb. 27, 1895: 11.

12

Patience Rewarded

As a congregational leader, Samuel Zug (1831-1926) favored mercy and patience rather than rigid discipline. The Chiques, Pennsylvania, congregation, where he was elder, once decided to purchase hymnals for worship. Not all members agreed with the plans and, at the next council meeting, it was decided not to use the books.

Zug wisely let the hymnals remain unused on the ministers' table for several months. Then one morning his brother, the chief objector to using the new hymnals, happened to pick one up and lined a hymn from it. S. R. Zug's patience was rewarded. There was no more opposition to the new songbooks in the Chiques congregation.

The Brethren Encyclopedia. Philadelphia, Pa., and Oak Brook, Ill.: The Brethren Encyclopedia, Inc., 1983-84: 642 (sidebar).

Saylor, Guy, ed. *History of the Church of the Brethren, Eastern Pennsylvania, 1915-1965*, n.d.

13
The Twin Preachers

Known among the Brethren as the twin preachers, Joseph and Henry Longanecker were noted both for their remarkable physical resemblance and for their similar pulpit methods. Their early careers were parallel, if not identical.

Born in Potsdam, Ohio, in 1848, they were married the same year (1869), united with the church in the same year (1870), and elected to the ministry in the same year (1882). But they were called to different areas of ministry. Joseph remained in southern Ohio, where he served the Prices Creek congregation for thirty-four years. Henry spent sixteen years in North Dakota and Washington, returning to Ohio in 1916. Henry died in 1920, Joseph in 1927.

The Brethren Encyclopedia. Philadelphia, Pa., and Oak Brook, Ill.: The Brethren Encyclopedia, Inc., 1983-84: 756 (sidebar).

Garst, Jesse O., ed. *History of the Church of the Brethren of the Southern District of Ohio*. Dayton: Otterbein Press, 1921.

14
Communion Bread

The General Conference of the Dunkard Brethren Church in 1944 recommended a recipe for baking Communion bread that contains "neither leaven or seasoning." The recipe, intended to serve fifty to sixty communicants, calls for the following ingredients: Six standard measuring cups of flour, or 1½ lbs.; ½ lb. butter, preferably unsalted; one pint of whole milk. The instructions are: "Rub butter and flour together as for pastry; add milk; knead until small blisters appear. Roll 3/8 inch thick on baking sheets; mark in strips one inch wide; prick closely with fork; bake in moderate oven at 375 degrees." Similar recipes appear in the *Inglenook Cook Book* (1911) and *Granddaughter's Inglenook Cookbook* (1942).

According to traditional practices still followed in some Brethren congregations, a consecration service precedes the baking of the bread by sisters of the church, usually wives of deacons. After preparing the dough in a dough tray, they divide it into smaller units for kneading, then roll it flat so that it can be ruled off into narrow strips. A three-pronged fork is used to prick holes in the dough, often with five holes across to represent the five wounds of Christ on the cross. After baking, the bread can be broken into strips for use in the Communion service.

The Brethren Encyclopedia. Philadelphia, Pa., and Oak Brook, Ill.: The Brethren Encyclopedia, Inc., 1983-84: 1293 (sidebar).
General Conference Minutes, Dunkard Brethren Church, 1927-1975.
Granddaughter's Inglenook Cookbook. Elgin, Ill.: Brethren Press, 1942.
Inglenook Cook Book, Elgin, Ill.: Brethren Publishing House, 1911.

15

The Union Sunday School

When I was a boy, I spent several weeks each summer with relatives on a farm at Artemas in the southern part of Bedford County, Pennsylvania. At Artemas there was a small Brethren congregation that my grandfather, John Bennett, had served for many years in the free ministry. But age and blindness now kept him from being active, so Brethren services were held every other week, when a visiting preacher could serve.

A short distance up the road from the Brethren church was a small Christian church (later to be known as Congregational-Christian, and now as the United Church of Christ), where a visiting pastor of the Christian church preached on the alternate Sundays. What made the cooperative arrangement work so smoothly was a union Sunday school that served all the "Christians" and the "Brethren" in the Artemas community. Though the setting for worship changed from Sunday to Sunday, the attendance remained about the same. The Christian folk came regularly to the Brethren service, and the Brethren were just as faithful at the Christian service.

The union Sunday school had one set of officers and, for the most part, a common treasury; lesson materials came from both denominations; offerings found their way to outreach programs supported by both groups; members took advantage of conferences and leadership events sponsored by each denomination; and when they held a vacation Bible school, its leadership came from both churches.

Since Grandfather Bennett was the only resident minister, he often served as pastor for families in need, conducting most of the weddings and funerals. I recall several times when, dressed in plain Brethren garb, he would be seated in one of the church yards or at a neighborhood gathering, always treated as a local patriarch by people whose voices he recognized even if he could not see them.

I doubt if Grandfather, or most of the Artemas people, ever heard the word *ecumenical*, but they were not reluctant to think of themselves as the people of God in the Artemas area. It wasn't that Grandfather was indifferent to sectarian arguments. He had shared in all the age-old controversies about beliefs and practices, and he did not hesitate to take on any advocate for single immersion. With vigor, even in his old age, he could make the scriptural case for trine immersion.

Maybe it was sheer necessity, rather than an understanding of ecumenicity, that brought Brethren and Christians together in Artemas. But in any case, for a period of more than thirty years, they studied the Bible and worshiped together under one label and then another, while they lived side-by-side in one neighborhood.

Wright, Lee-Lani, ed. *Church of the Brethren Handbook on Church Unity*. Elgin, Ill.: Brethren Press, 1988: 28.

16

Wrestling with the Devil

William Sevits (1812-1889) was an elder in the Berlin congregation in western Pennsylvania. A large, strong man, he won many wrestling matches. His grandson Fred W. Brant tells about an incident that occurred around 1872 when Sevits was holding evangelistic meetings in a mountainous area of Somerset County, where rough characters had a habit of breaking up revival services.

On the third evening of this revival meeting, after the Elder read the Scripture and had announced his sermon topic, a strange thing happened. Elder Sevits announced that his topic was "Casting Out Devils." Two tall, strong, rough-looking ruffians came to the front of the church and stood facing the pulpit. One of them, well over six feet [tall], held up a whiskey bottle and offered Elder Sevits a drink from his bottle in the presence of the whole congregation. . . .

On this challenge, Sevits stepped down in front to where the two men were standing. He quickly grabbed the troublemakers by the necks and bumped their heads together with such a thump that they both collapsed before the people on the floor unconscious. The Elder then, without saying a word, stooped down and took them each by an arm and pulled them outside the church and dumped them on the ground. . . .

Upon reentering the church, he said: 'I did not expect to literally demonstrate my text and sermon topic this evening.' He walked to the platform and preached such a sermon that no one present even budged an inch. The church was so startled to see a Dunker preacher in such action, and yet they all knew that he was firm in his convictions of peaceful living. . . .

The next day the same two men came to see Elder Sevits, pleading that he would not bring any legal charges against them for their actions the previous evening in the church. He told them that he would forgive them on one condition: that they each attend the rest of the revival meetings, every night.

[The two men never missed a meeting during the remaining services. Both were converted and reputed to have become elders in the church. K.M.]

The Brethren Encyclopedia. Philadelphia, Pa., and Oak Brook, Ill.: The Brethren Encyclopedia, Inc., 1983-84: 1103-04 (sidebar).

Cooper, H. Austin. *Two Centuries of Brothersvalley Church of the Brethren, 1762-1962*. Privately printed, 1962.

17

Love Feast at Knob Creek

In his book of memories of growing up in the late nineteenth century in Tennessee, Reuel Pritchett, with the assistance of Dale Aukerman, tells vivid stories of love feasts he attended as a boy at the Knob Creek church in Tennessee.

The Knob Creek church was the hub of the whole country religiously. It was the center; all the other churches and denominations regulated their preaching hour and Sunday by what we had done. We had the ups on it; the first Sunday in the month was the Brethren's day. Back then we had preaching only once a month, and the other churches too. We had good crowds, the largest of anybody in the country. People who wasn't Brethren or maybe didn't belong to any church would often refer to Knob Creek as their church and attend meeting there. On love feast occasions, everybody in the whole community, Brethren and non-Brethren alike, made preparations for feeding and lodging the big crowd. There would be a couple of beefs killed and everybody spoke for twenty pounds or so.

Invariably two or three men would preach. They'd be at it for an hour and a half or more. One would open the service and one would preach and one would close. The first brother would line a hymn and read some scripture and preach down through it; that-a-way he got his say in. He'd set down, and the next brother would really take a text and preach. Then he'd set down, and the third brother would close the service; he'd preach awhile.

But there was no advance decision about who was a-gonna preach. With the home preachers, of which there was three or four who lived at Knob Creek, it was sort of a gentlemen's understanding that they take it in turns. But our church being the center of the brotherhood in Tennessee, we'd have visiting preachers from a distance, often two or three or four of them. And then the weighty question arose, who's a-gonna preach? Of course, our Brethren would "prefer one another," extending the privilege to the visiting preachers. But there'd be an argument between the several of them. I've seen them elbow each other, talk about it, pass the word along, line another hymn and sing it while they were deciding. And when one did rise, he might have to throw in a lot of adjectives and other material to give his mind a chance to think. . . .

In those days I heard a number of great preachers—H. C. Early, Andrew Hutchinson, S. J. Smith, George C. Bowman—and many another. When I was eight years old, H. C. Early preached a revival at Knob Creek. I had a little day book and I set down the scriptures he preached on and some of his subjects. But it went along until C. H. Diehl, a Tennessean, a good man but not a big preacher, was holding a revival. On the night of January 5, I was strangely moved. He preached a powerful sermon, I thought; it went through me. They sung that hymn,

I will arise and go to Jesus
He will embrace me in His arms,
In the arms of my dear Savior,
Though there are ten thousand foes.

It's a masterpiece. It raised me. I walked down the aisle and gave an old saint my hand, and six others with me did the same. That was in the old log church on Knob Creek back in 1900.

Pritchett, Reuel, with Dale Aukerman. *On the Ground Floor of Heaven*. Elgin, Ill.: Brethren Press, 1980. Excerpts.

18

Preaching on a Cattle Boat

Since there were a number of ministers who volunteered to serve as "cowboys" for the United Nations Relief and Rehabilitation Administration (UNRRA), regular worship services were usually held on the ships. These services were attended by crew members as well as Brethren volunteers. Reuel Pritchett (1884–1974) gives an account of a return trip to America from Greece.

On our return voyage, I made me a church on deck, right where one of the horse stables had been. I took a hose and flushed it all out nice and clean. It had open cracks like a crib. I got planks we'd used for partitions, scrubbed them all up, slipped them into the cracks, and made raised seats all the way back. I made me a stand and took a towel out of my grip for a spread on the stand. We was out on the deck, and the wind would be so heavy I'd have to weight the towel down with something, or my Bible and all would have been blown away. So I polished up some ammunition cartridges that I'd secured from under the rubble of waterfront warehouses in Athens and perched them on the spread for vases to hold it down tight.

There we would have open forum. We discussed everything. We had a big time. And I would preach. (I had preached going over, too, but without the deck chapel.) I wore work clothes, but when I went to preach, I put on my clergy. I washed and dressed and appeared as stately as I knew how to do. I had the high-ranking officers and the reprobate old seamen and the soldiers we were hauling back instead of horses. They all came to church, and I unloaded on them. I preached with as much emphasis as I would anywhere. One profane old seaman said to me, "Mr. Pritchett, this is the first time we ever had any religion on this boat."

Pritchett, Reuel, with Dale Aukerman. *On the Ground Floor of Heaven*. Elgin, Ill.: Brethren Press, 1980.

19

Lessons Learned at Love Feast

Andrew W. Cordier, who helped draft the charter of the United Nations and who for seventeen years served as one of its top officials, once told an interviewer that he received his first world view at the Brethren love feast. Inez Long quotes Cordier as saying in 1960:

> Utter sincerity, utter fairness, and utter integrity are basic to communication, and I first learned them as prior conditions to coming to the love feast tables. At these tables, after applying the rules of Matthew 18, the Brethren dramatize the idea of brotherhood under God.
>
> I saw these concepts acted out before my eyes, by people I loved and trusted, from the time I could remember. The ideas stayed with me. . . . Such concepts of brotherhood at the conference tables of the United Nations give peace a fighting chance.

M. R. Zigler recalled an occasion when, "in the presence of Dag Hammarskjöld, a visiting delegation of the World Council of Churches Central Committee, and representatives of the United Nations, [Cordier] said he found that his basic teaching came from what is known as the 'love feast' of the Church of the Brethren to which he belonged."

The Brethren Encyclopedia. Philadelphia, Pa., and Oak Brook, Ill.: The Brethren Encyclopedia, Inc., 1983-84: 765 (sidebar).
Long, Inez. "Down-to-Earth Peacemaker." *Gospel Messenger*, March 12, 1960: 4-7.

The Scrappers Get Together

—peace and justice

20

A Short and Sincere Declaration

Faced with increasing pressures from many of their neighbors to take up arms against the British, leaders of Pennsylvania Mennonites and Brethren submitted a petition to the General Assembly on November 7, 1775, setting forth the principles of conscience that would guide nonresisters in their response.

To our Honorable Assembly, and all others in high or low station of administration, and to all friends and inhabitants of this country, to whose sight this may come, be they English or German.

Further we find ourselves to be indebted to be thankful to our late worthy Assembly, for their giving so good an advice in these troublesome times to all ranks of people in Pennsylvania.

The advice to those who do not find freedom of conscience to take up arms, that they ought to be helpful to those who are in need and distressed circumstances, we receive with cheerfulness toward all men of what station they may be—it being our principle to feed the hungry and give the thirsty drink. We have dedicated ourselves to serve all men in every thing that can be helpful to the preservation of men's lives, but we find no freedom in giving, or doing, or assisting in anything by which men's lives are destroyed or hurt. . . .

We are always ready, according to Christ's command to Peter, to pay the tribute, that we may offend no man, and so we are willing to pay taxes, and to render unto Caesar all those things that are Caesar's and to God those things that are God's, although we think ourselves very weak to give God his due honor, He being a spirit and life, and we only dust and ashes.

We are also willing to be subject to the higher powers, and to give in the manner Paul directs us: "For he does not bear the sword in vain; he is the servant of God, to execute his wrath on the wrongdoer."

This testimony we lay down before our worthy Assembly, and all other persons in government, letting them know that we are thankful as above mentioned, and that we are not at liberty in conscience to take up arms to conquer our enemies, but rather to pray to God, who has power in heaven and on earth, for us and them. . . .

Our small gift, which we have given, we give to those who have power over us, that we may not offend them, as Christ taught us by the tribute penny.

We heartily pray that God would govern all hearts of our rulers, be they high or low, to mediate those good things which will pertain to our and their happiness.

The above declaration, signed by a number of elders and teachers of the Society of Mennonites and some of the German Baptists, presented to the Honorable House of Assembly on the 7th day of November 1775, was most graciously received.

Durnbaugh, Donald F., ed. *The Brethren in Colonial America*. Elgin, Ill.: Brethren Press, 1967.

Martin, Harold S. and Dennis D. Martin. "Pennsylvania." *The Brethren Encyclopedia*. Philadelphia, Pa., and Oak Brook, Ill.: The Brethren Encyclopedia, Inc., 1983-84.

21
True Patriotism

John Kline heard the distant thunder of cannon in 1849. It could have been a premonition of the Civil War that would test his character and eventually take his life, but actually it was merely a celebration of George Washington's birthday. Kline had no objection to such public displays of patriotic feelings, but he was stimulated to think of a different sort of patriotism. So he wrote in his diary for Thursday, February 22, 1849:

> I have a somewhat higher conception of true patriotism than can be represented by the firing of guns which give forth nothing but meaningless sound. I am glad, however, that these guns report harmless sound, and nothing more. If some public speakers would do the same, it might be better for both them and their hearers. My highest conception of patriotism is found in the man who loves the Lord his God with all his heart and his neighbor as himself. Out of these affections spring the subordinate love for one's country; love truly virtuous for one's companion and children, relatives and friends; and in its most comprehensive sense takes in the whole human family. Were this love universal, the word

> patriotism, in its specific sense, meaning such a love for one's country as makes its possessors ready and willing to take up arms in its defense, might be appropriately expunged from every national vocabulary.

Many years later John Kline heard the thunder of cannon again, this time at Mt. Jackson, Virginia, on the day that he and other prisoners were to be moved to New Market. This was no birthday celebration. General Jackson's army was retreating. Federal troops were expected.

Kline and two others were released from the guard house on Good Friday, 1862. He would be home by Easter to live for two more years and then to die as a patriot "who love[d] the Lord his God with all his heart and his neighbor as himself."

The Brethren Encyclopedia. Philadelphia, Pa., and Oak Brook, Ill.: The Brethren Encyclopedia, Inc., 1983-84: 702 (sidebar).

Funk, Benjamin, *Life of John Kline.* Elgin, Ill.: Brethren Publishing House, 1900.

22

Arrested for Preaching the Gospel

How could preaching a sermon on an assigned text from Isaiah ever be cause for arrest? Such was the experience of Samuel Garber in 1858, when he preached on Isaiah 58:6 at a Presbyterian church in eastern Tennessee. Garber, a former Tennessee resident who was visiting from Illinois, described the dramatic event in a report to *The Gospel Visitor* in April 1859.

> I attended at the time appointed and found a large concourse assembled. I took the . . . text and delivered a discourse. I spoke of the yoke and the bondage of sin in general terms, and of temperance, justice, and judgment to come, and particularly against oppression in every shape and form. I held forth the law of love, mercy, and truth; showed that there was a time coming when every yoke of sin would be broken, intemperance banished from our sphere, oppression cease, contention, strife and wars would be at an end; love, peace, good-will, union and fellowship would universally prevail throughout the whole earth, etc.

Preaching in a Tavern

> About the close of my discourse, I said that among the yokes and oppressions might be named that of slavery . . . .

Here was the beginning of Samuel Garber's troubles—the application of his text to slavery. Immediately another minister announced that he would show that the text had no reference to African slavery. A newspaper article accused Garber of having the audacity to deliver an abolition sermon in the presence of master and slave. Garber was confronted with threats of lynch law, of being tarred and feathered and ridden out of town on a rail. A few weeks later he was arrested with a state warrant for preaching an abolition sermon. Garber refused to appear on a Sunday, but the next day he was set free on $500 bail "to appear in the next term of court." Brethren in the area persuaded Garber, a Brethren minister, to leave the state, because they feared further agitation might lead to violence. They paid Garber's forfeited bail money.

Though Garber learned later that many in his audience supported his stand, he eventually had to pay court costs and lawyer's fees amounting to $234. He commented, "A pretty round sum to be paid for preaching the gospel! Where is the boasted liberty of the pulpit and the press?"

The Scrappers Get Together

The Gospel Visitor not only told his story but encouraged readers to share the expense of his trial.

The Brethren Encyclopedia. Philadelphia, Pa., and Oak Brook, Ill.: The Brethren Encyclopedia, Inc., 1983-84: 1-2 (sidebar).
The Gospel Visitor, April 1859: 121-23.
The Gospel Visitor, September 1859: 283-85.

23

Quantrill's Raid—A Most Dastardly Episode

Dr. Elmer Leroy Craik, Brethren historian and professor of history at McPherson and Juniata Colleges, describes Civil War incidents in which a band of guerillas led by William C. Quantrill gathered up three hundred desperadoes one day and killed 150 innocent people in just a few hours. Always so mild mannered and precise in his writing, Craik uses such terms as "a dastardly episode," "the drunken and infuriated band of desperadoes," and "vicious intention" to describe the attack on Lawrence, Kansas, and the farm of Brother Jacob Ulrich.

On August 21, 1863, there occurred at Lawrence one of the most dastardly episodes of the whole war. William C. Quantrill, a guerilla of more or less notoriety, had for some time nursed a grievance against this free-state town. Early on the morning of the day mentioned, he swooped down on the defenseless town. In a few hours about one hundred fifty persons were killed and from one to two million dollars worth of property was destroyed. Vengeance had at last been visited upon the hated "Yankees."

The drunken and infuriated band of desperadoes left burning Lawrence late in the forenoon, going almost directly south from the present site of the University of Kansas on Mount Oread. Dinner time found them at the well-ordered farm of prosperous Deacon Jacob Ulrich, nine miles south of Lawrence. The aged brother was not aware of their malicious intentions, but two of his sons, John and Daniel, and a son-in-law, Joseph Shively, divined their fell purposes and rescued the unoffending deacon and his wife. The Quantrill band helped themselves to all the edibles to be had. Then the house was fired, many valuable records and papers perishing therein. The fine twenty-five-hundred-dollar barn with its well-filled bins and mow went up in smoke. Leaving the buildings in ruins, the raiders set out toward the river, hoping to escape thence into Missouri. John Ulrich wished to pursue the fleeing mob, but the better counsel of his father prevailed, the latter insisting firmly upon an adherence to the well-known non-resistant principles of the church.

The guerillas also brought distress to the quiet home of Elder Abraham Rothrock, who lived south of the Ulrich farm. It appears that Elder Rothrock, warned of the approach of the long-haired ruffians, had gone to hide in the cornfield, but concerned that his wife and daughter were being mistreated by the men, he returned to the house. Taking a stand near the open cellar door, he attempted to reason with the guerillas. Elder Rothrock was shot three times and thrown into the cellar with the remark: "That's the way we treat all d____d old preachers." The house was then fired and the band moved on south.

As they left, one of the men, a former neighbor named Campbell, remained to help care for the wounded elder. Neighbor Daniel Ulrich was also present and helped carry the victim up out of the cellar. Brother Rothrock received wounds in his shoulder, chin, and the back of his neck, but he survived.

Through the ordeal, Rothrock never deviated from his conscientious principles. While he was still lying in bed, a Baptist preacher named Tucker called and, expecting to discover a weakening in the elder's views, asked him, "Mr. Rothrock, what would you do if you had those men [the guerillas] in your power now?"

Quick as a flash the prostrate man replied: "I would convert every one of them."

"Well," said the neighbor, "that beats my religion."

Craik, Elmer L. *History of the Church of the Brethren in Kansas*. Privately printed, 1922.

24

The Scrappers Get Together

It took a general in the army to touch a sore point in the peace witness of the Brethren. During World War I, the Brethren made their case on behalf of conscientious objection to General Crowder in Washington, D.C. When Crowder asked the Brethren delegation how many divisions there were in the denomination, W. J. Swigart, head of the delegation, confessed to the number of divisions in the church. The general's response was: "You are pretty good scrappers for a peace people after all."

By the time World War II came along, the Brethren record on divisions was no better, but at least the problem of dealing with government was recognized by all Brethren. Thus, representatives of five Brethren groups—the Old Order German Baptists, the Brethren Church, the Fellowship of Grace Brethren Church, the Dunkard Brethren Church, and the Church of the Brethren—came together at the Brethren Publishing House in Elgin, Illinois, to decide on a course of action as they faced the military draft.

Rufus D. Bowman, at that time president of Bethany Biblical Seminary in Chicago, presided at the meeting.

He began by inviting ideas and proposals from each group. Brother Jacob W. Skiles, who served ten times as foreman (moderator) of the Old Order group, at first declined to suggest any ideas or make any proposals. He said, "We're from the country and don't know what to do."

Rufus Bowman looked around and observed that many others were from the country and said, "Please don't feel so humble. I'm from the country too."

"Yes, I know," replied Skiles. "But we just came from the country this morning."

The Brethren from the country and others from the city cooperated and began a process that involved many meetings with government that resulted in an extensive program for conscientious objectors from every church background. Brother Skiles later made many trips to Washington, served as a counselor to conscientious objectors in his church, and was highly respected by church and government leaders.

Another remarkable testimony to the spirit of cooperation among Brethren groups is *The Brethren Encyclopedia*, a three-volume reference work published in 1983 and 1984. The editorial board is composed of two representatives from each group, and all five Brethren groups are represented on its governing board. The encyclopedia board continues to develop other publications of mutual Brethren interest and sponsors informal and unofficial study conferences that provide an open forum for the discussion of issues of concern to all Brethren.

Wright, Lee-Lani, ed. *Church of the Brethren Handbook on Church Unity*. Elgin, Ill.: Brethren Press, 1988. Adapted.

Miller, J. E. *The Story of Our Church*. Elgin, Ill.: Brethren Publishing House, 1941, 1957.

Minnich, H. Spenser. "Farewell to a Friendly Old Building." *Gospel Messenger*, May 9, 1959: 15,18.

25

Peace Witness at a Court-Martial

During World War I, Maurice A. Hess, a member of the Old German Baptist Church, suffered severe treatment, including solitary confinement, at Fort Leavenworth, Kansas, because of his peace convictions. At his court-martial, he offered this eloquent statement of his position.

As a young man, life and its hopes and freedom and opportunities for service are sweet to me. I want to go out into the world and make use of what little talent I may have acquired by long and laborious study.

But I know that I dare not purchase these things at the price of eternal condemnation. I know the teaching of Christ, my Savior. He taught us to resist not evil, to love our enemies, to bless them that curse us, and do good to them that hate us. Not only did he teach this, but he also practiced it in Gethsemane, before Pilate, and on Calvary. We would indeed be hypocrites and base traitors to our profession if we would be unwilling to bear the taunts and jeers of a sinful world, and imprisonment, and torture or death, rather than to participate in war and military service. We know that obedience to Christ will gain for us the glorious prize of eternal life. We cannot yield, we cannot compromise, we must suffer.

Two centuries ago our people were driven out of Germany by religious persecution, and they accepted the invitation of William Penn to come to his colony where they might enjoy the blessing of religious liberty which he promised them. This religious liberty was later confirmed by the Constitution of Pennsylvania and the Constitution of the United States.

If the authorities now see fit to change those fundamental documents and take away our privilege of living in accordance with the teaching of the scriptures of God, then we have no course but to endure persecution as true soldiers of Christ.

If I have committed anything worthy of bonds or death, I do not refuse to suffer or die.

I pray God for strength to remain faithful.

The Brethren Encyclopedia. Philadelphia, Pa., and Oak Brook, Ill.: The Brethren Encyclopedia, Inc., 1983-84: 1371 (sidebar).

26
Symbol of Service

It began with a photograph taken to illustrate an Annual Conference theme for the Church of the Brethren. It soon developed into a graphic symbol used to identify the purposes and program of Brethren Service.

The theme for the 1939 Annual Conference was "Brethren in Reality." The photographic illustration showed J. E. Miller, editor and historian, offering to C. D. Bonsack, for many years executive secretary of the General Mission Board, a cup originally used in Communion services in the Germantown church. E. G. Hoff was the photographer. The picture was soon adapted for a related purpose when the Brethren Service Committee (BSC) was formed in 1941 and needed a symbol to interpret the biblical and historical roots of its timely work. The sharing hands, giving and receiving "a cup of water in Christ's name" (Matt. 10:42; Mark 9:41), were placed in the context of the cross of Christ and in a circle that signified wholeness. The design soon received wide circulation.

During the years of World War II, Brethren Service stamps with this symbol often served as an alternative to the purchase of war bonds and stamps. Income from the stamps supported the work of the BSC. At the same time, a Brethren Service cup, crafted in Oregon of myrtlewood, was made available for use on family tables and on church worship centers to promote offerings for peace and service.

The Brethren Encyclopedia. Philadelphia, Pa., and Oak Brook, Ill.: The Brethren Encyclopedia, Inc., 1983-84: 201 (sidebar).

Brandt, Harry A. "The Story of a Symbol." *Gospel Messenger,* March 8, 1941: 3.

27
Creative Pacifism

"These are the years of destruction; we offer against them the creative act." The years of destruction were the years of World War II. The creative act was offered by conscientious objectors in Civilian Public Service (CPS), especially those who helped form a fine arts group at Camp No. 56, a Brethren-sponsored unit at Waldport, Oregon. The fine arts group was described as "a venture of CPS writers, artists, actors, and musicians devoted to the furtherance of pacifist creative expression."

Although the Waldport group produced plays, offered a concert series, exhibited paintings, and encouraged crafts, members excelled in printing and illustrating their original literary works. In 1944, under the imprint of the Untide Press, they used a small hand press to publish collections of poetry by Jacob Sloan, Glen Coffield, and William Everson, the director of the project.

Everson, who later became a Dominican lay brother and wrote under the name Brother Antonius, won national recognition for his poetry and printing. In an interview published in 1971, Everson said, "At Waldport we proposed an arts project and were accepted.

On the basis of this, we began to attract artists from camps all over the country. . . . Actually a good deal of what later happened in the San Francisco scene had its origins right there in Waldport."

The Brethren Encyclopedia. Philadelphia, Pa., and Oak Brook, Ill.: The Brethren Encyclopedia, Inc., 1983-84: 317 (sidebar).

Eisan, Leslie. *Pathways of Peace.* Elgin, Ill.: Brethren Publishing House, 1948.

Enberg, Craig. "Everson at Waldport." *Brethren Life and Thought,* Vol. XIX (1974): 135-140.

28

The Smokejumpers

"Smokejumper" was the term applied to a small number of conscientious objectors who served as parachute firefighters during World War II. They prepared by learning how to pack and repair a chute, control a fire, and offer first aid. However well rehearsed, their seven practice jumps could not quite prevent a feeling of apprehension when they lined up for their turns, ready to jump from a plane circling over a recently spotted forest fire.

The smokejumpers were members of one of the most dramatic and well-publicized Civilian Public Service units. Their base camp, number 103, located near Missoula, Montana, was administered by the Mennonite Central Committee, but it drew applicants from Brethren and Friends camps as well, about twenty from each agency (sixty in all) for the first season in 1943. Altogether, in three seasons (1943–1945), about 240 men joined the unit and prepared to be sent out in squads of eight to fifteen men to strategic points in Montana, Idaho, Oregon, and Washington.

When fires in these areas were observed from lookout stations, the smokejumpers would suit up and be prepared to jump as soon as the spotter plane had picked a landing place for the smokejumpers. They faced their greatest danger in landing, but most escaped no more serious injury than a sprained ankle or a broken bone. In most instances they were able to extinguish fires before they grew out of control.

The Brethren Encyclopedia. Philadelphia, Pa., and Oak Brook, Ill.: The Brethren Encyclopedia, Inc., 1983-84: 337 (sidebar).

Eisan, Leslie. *Pathways of Peace.* Elgin, Ill.: Brethren Publishing House, 1948.

Gingrich, Melvin. *Service for Peace.* Akron, Pa.: Mennonite Central Committee, 1949.

29

To Help Others as We Were Helped

The refugees in Austria after World War II noticed something different about the Brethren woman Helena Kruger. Not only did she speak more languages than most American workers (Russian, German, Dutch, Polish), but she also evidently understood how refugees felt and what they experienced.

They were right about Helena Kruger, for she had once been a refugee—at the time of World War I. Knowing about starvation firsthand, she said, "Starvation is a terrible thing. Those who have not experienced it do not know. Field mice, dead horses, and whatever you can find can be eaten when hunger is keen enough." And Helena knew about being displaced, traveling in strange countries, living in refugee camps. She also appreciated what it meant for her family when the Mennonite Central Committee helped them resettle in the United States.

So when the Krugers heard from Brethren Service workers about the plight of European refugees following World War II, they arranged their lives so that at least Helena could assist. Her husband said, "If the church had not helped us to come to America, we would be homeless a second time." Helena was soon ready to go back to Europe as a volunteer, first in Belgium, then in Austria, Italy, and finally to Greece, when her husband could go along. She told her friends, "We wanted to help others as we had been helped."

The Brethren Encyclopedia. Philadelphia, Pa., and Oak Brook, Ill.: The Brethren Encyclopedia, Inc., 1983-84: 708 (sidebar).
Kruger, Helena. "A Twentieth-Century Pilgrimage." *Messenger*, April 15, 1971: 12-15.

30

A Synoptic View of BVS Beginnings

In 1998 Brethren Volunteer Service (BVS) celebrates its fiftieth anniversary. Stories of how this popular program was launched in Colorado Springs in 1948 vary significantly. At the time of its thirty-fifth anniversary, Becky Baile, a BVSer with journalistic experience, who later served in Poland, gave this first account.

A 4-foot-10 Manchester College sophomore, Ted Chambers, delegate from Michigan to the 1948 Annual Conference, watched for the signal. When moderator Calvert N. Ellis stuck up his thumb, it meant Ted was to race to an orange crate strategically situated before a microphone and introduce a new business item not on the regular agenda.

The plan Chambers proposed came from Brethren youth concerned about military conscription. It called for immediate action by the Church of the Brethren General Board to launch a volunteer service program with financial support from the entire denomination. Conference unanimously accepted the statement, which instituted Brethren Volunteer Service. . . .

BVS began from dreams of well-known Brethren, including Dan West. He helped the youth behind the scenes in 1948 to draw up the plan for volunteer service. Initially, BVS training was three months in length. But in 1949, units were shortened to eight weeks (later increased to nine) because eager volunteers wanted to get to their projects.

The first BVS orientation unit gathered at New Windsor, Maryland, but because of its size, it was divided into sections. Some volunteers went to Camp Harmony, a Church of the Brethren camp, while others remained at the New Windsor Service Center.

Baile, Becky. "Thirty-five Years of Brethren Volunteer Service." *Messenger*, December 1983: 12.

From Donald Durnbaugh's biography of M. R. Zigler, Pragmatic Prophet, *comes this report of youth praying over a year's time for a volunteer youth program.*

The immediate origin of BVS was Zigler's powerful address to the assembled Brethren youth at the Orlando, Florida, Annual Conference, in 1947. His firsthand accounts of the suffering he had seen in Europe shook his hearers. His message was electrifying. It shocked the youth into a state of horror; dismay and soul-searching followed, then the question, "What can we do?" The decision was to begin praying and wait for an answer. A twenty-four-hour prayer vigil was spontaneously organized, lasting throughout the conference. In modified form, it was perpetuated through the following year.

During that time, some of these young people worked with peace caravans; that initiative had emerged from a powerful work camp experience in Salina, Kansas, in 1947. [Caravans] involved volunteers touring Brethren congregations; a carload of young people would visit for several days to a week, presenting programs and working extensively with the young people. Others at the work camp pledged to give sacrificially from their wages to support the caravans.

As these young people came to the 1948 Conference, they decided to hold prayer vigils before each business meeting. Their primary concern was that the church provide a structure that would allow young members of the church to do something positive for peace and not simply say "no" to war. With the behind-the-scenes advice of Dan West and some others, the young people prepared a query to present to the delegates at the conference. Breaking with polity procedures, the question was accepted as a new item of business and then adopted by the voting body, which then delegated the new program to a surprised Brethren Service Commission for implementation.

Durnbaugh, Donald F. *Pragmatic Prophet: The Life of M. R. Zigler.* Elgin, Ill.: On Earth Peace Assembly, Inc., Church of the Brethren General Board, 1989.

Another group given credit for the formation of BVS is the National Youth Cabinet, youth and their leaders who planned activities that opened the way for more official support of volunteer service.

Because of wartime conditions, youth and district leaders had just participated in a delegate conference for youth, held instead of a total Brethren youth conference. Fresh from this meeting, the National Youth Cabinet met in Colorado Springs, primed with new ideas for making their youth activities more successful. In their prayer cell groups, they considered the prospects for BVS; changed the name of their youth organization from Brethren Young People's Department (BYPD) to Brethren Youth Fellowship (BYF); and proposed a new name for their youth publication, calling it *Horizons for Youth* instead of *Our Young People*. National Youth Director, Don Snider, recorded the events and decisions of these busy days in a diary. He relates that "W. Harold Row, head of Brethren Service, recognized all the problems that needed to be faced in developing a program that would not only channel the idealism of our young people but which would also contribute significantly to relieve suffering and bear a witness for peace and justice in the name of Christ. But those of us who were in the meetings knew also that Harold would do everything in his power to make this program succeed."

31

College Honors a Life of Faith

It was in the 1960s that some college pranksters managed quite successfully one night to put a cow on the third floor of the Administration Building of Manchester College. Stories vary about who was responsible, how they managed to pull it off, how the administration reacted, and how the culprits were disciplined. All reports say the cow was pregnant at the time and had a premature delivery in which she lost her calf.

Without knowing which students were involved, we can assume that some were present some twenty-five or thirty years later at the academic services held in April 1995 at Manchester College when Heifer Project International was awarded an honorary degree of Doctor of Humane Letters.

Faith, the Guernsey cow who was the first animal offered for Heifers for Relief (HFR), was given by Virgil Mock in response to an appeal by Dan West at a Northern Indiana men's meeting. Faith was fed and cared for by Clair Stine, whose father offered to furnish the feed until she could be sent overseas. Along with sixteen other cows, Faith was dedicated in a worship service at the Rock Run Church in Indiana before being transported to Mobile, Alabama, where she was shipped on July 14, 1944, to Puerto Rico by the Heifer Project committee working in cooperation with the Farm Security Administration. There she found a home with Señor Meliton Lind Lopez of Barrio Ward Mediania in the Rio Grande, whose family of ten children needed the milk she could supply. In her lifetime Faith produced nine calves, all of them males. She had several granddaughters who could form a small dairy herd for Lopez.

It has been fifty years since Faith began that first journey. Since that time millions of chickens and thousands of other animals have traveled to more than ninety countries and several states within the U.S., and the gift goes on and on.

The Brethren Encyclopedia. Philadelphia, Pa., and Oak Brook, Ill.: The Brethren Encyclopedia, Inc., 1983-84: 594 (sidebar).

Yoder, Glee. *Passing on the Gift: The Story of Dan West.* Brethren Press, 1978, 1995.

32

The Dunkers and UNRRA

It was 1945 and, according to *Time* magazine, the Baltimore stockyards were full of livestock, and an empty ship waited in the harbor, but there was no one to herd the animals on to the ship and overseas to the hungry survivors of World War II. The United Nations Relief and Rehabilitation Administration (UNRRA) didn't know what to do.

That is, until Benjamin G. Bushong, a member of the Church of the Brethren, entered the picture to cut the red tape. It seems that Brother Bushong, in an effort to send cattle overseas as part of the Brethren relief program, had run into a snag. Like the UNRRA, he had cattle, for Dunkers from the city had raised money for calves and feed, and Dunkers from the country had fattened the calves. But the Church of the Brethren relief program had no ships. Brother Bushong made a deal with UNRRA: he would find livestock hustlers if UNRRA would provide shipping space.

Benjamin Bushong, dairy farmer and cemetery owner, was successful in recruiting one hundred volunteer herders, who had to respond to only two questions: "Who are you? What can you do?" As the ships set sail for various ports in Europe, pacifist Bushong is quoted as saying: "Perhaps shootin' isn't the only way out of this world mess."

Time magazine, July 23, 1945.

Reuel Pritchett was one of several volunteers who traveled to Greece with a boatload of horses. Pritchett was a farmer, pastor, and elder of the French Broad congregation in Tennessee. With his customary Brethren garb, a long, trimmed beard, and a black broad-brimmed hat, he was a commanding personality. This is how he remembers that trip.

I was once an ocean-roaming cowboy for horses. Several days after the close of World War II, we set sea at New Orleans with 350 horses and 10,000 tons of foods and feeds and relief goods to distribute in Greece. The name of our chubby freighter was the *Charles W. Wooster*. It was 485 feet long with a capacity of 10,500 tons, and we had it loaded to the hilt. The propeller on our ship was 18 feet in diameter and had a top speed of 71 revolutions per minute. . . .

Dan West, by the end of the war, was collecting a log of heifers and also calling for volunteer cowboys. I happened to be among the first volunteers. The Brethren made a contract with UNRRA and the United States government that we would help them take their horses over if they would let us have a ship to get our cargoes over. So our gang of cowboys went with horses, not heifers, and took orders from Washington.

I happened to be chosen captain of the sixteen men whose duties it was to take care of the horses. I wasn't supposed to work, but I worked all the time to keep the men a-working. Our ship wasn't built with horses in mind, and everything was unhandy. We had horses in the hull, in cages on the deck, even the upper deck, and in any corner we could find room to lodge one in. We fed them oats and hay twice daily, watered them in buckets that hung on the stable railings, and shoveled and windlassed and dumped overboard the old soiled bedding. . . .

A horse boat a day or so ahead of us hit a mine. Ship, cargo, and all the horses perished at sea, though the men were saved. As we sailed into those waters, we could see a horse now and then swimming forlornly, a little out of sight of Thessalonika. Swim and swim they would till they gave out and yielded to the sharks. . . .

Wandering through the streets of Thessalonika, I saw a scene that can stand for a thousand other scenes. A bunch of girls and women were sitting on the ground around a spigot. It was not running a trickle of water as big as a pencil. They had little cups, gourds, or anything, each one trying to ketch a sip of water.

Pritchett, Reuel, with Dale Aukerman. *On the Ground Floor of Heaven.* Elgin, Ill.: Brethren Press, 1980.

John Eller was also one of the seagoing cowboys. In a diary, he published his vivid impressions of delivering horses to Poland.

June 25, 1946
Up early. Did not have to feed the horses. They unloaded most of them last night. We lost 47 horses in all. . . . We got our shore passes around 9 a.m. . . .

Many people are walking the streets with no place to go. No home! No people! Nothing! If they are caught stealing, they are shot. Some have heard shots at night.

Preaching in a Tavern

We heard some today. Everything is all to pieces. An American Negro was shot tonight. The name of the little town where we docked is Newy Port. Some of the boys saw a little boy who stepped on a mine. He was bleeding pretty bad.

June 26, 1946

. . . We were in Danzig proper but a few minutes. It is very depressing. There is hardly a building standing and those that are have great holes in them. The stench is still terrible in some places. The population was reduced from 1,000,000 to 30,000 during the war. People live in filth, rubble, and haystacks. As our vet has said, "It is like going into the bowels of the earth."

Eller, John. *Wave Rider for Peace: A Diary of a Sea-going Cowboy to Poland—1946*, n.p., 1990.

33

Nonviolence Is the Only Way

On the first weekend in May 1970, Dean Kahler, a freshman at Kent State University in Ohio and a member of the Church of the Brethren, was at home when student demonstrations protesting the U.S. invasion of Cambodia broke out on the campus. The Monday following, while on his way to class, he was seriously injured as soldiers of the Ohio National Guard opened fire, fearing student protest would become violent. Four students were killed. Kahler dropped to the ground for cover, but a bullet entered his body, nearly killing him. He lost the use of his legs and had part of one lung removed.

The Center congregation, of which the Kahlers were members, and Brethren all over northern Ohio were supportive in the difficult months that followed. Because of the national publicity given the incident (one headline described Kahler as "the fifth victim of Kent State"), he received many "hate" letters accusing him of being a Communist radical. Influenced by his Brethren background, Kahler had earlier decided to be a conscientious objector and was opposed to the Vietnam War, but he had not been identified with the protest movement on the campus.

As a paraplegic Kahler made a remarkable comeback, even learning to play wheelchair basketball. Eventually he returned to his classes at Kent State where he received his B. S. degree in 1977. He joined with other injured students and the families of the four who had been killed in bringing a civil suit against the public officials they believed responsible for the shooting. Kahler told an interviewer in 1975: "We were taught as Brethren to love everybody, even those who smite you, or your enemies. I just try to keep remembering that all the time." Speaking at a memorial service at Kent State, he said, "Nonviolence is the only way."

The Brethren Encyclopedia. Philadelphia, Pa., and Oak Brook, Ill.: The Brethren Encyclopedia, Inc., 1983-84: 1306 (sidebar).

Royer, Howard. "Nonviolence Is the Only Way." *Messenger*, Jan.1, 1971: 2-5.

McGrory, Mary. "Outlook." *Messenger*, March 1974: 4-5.

Rosenberger, Mary Sue. "Kahler and Kent State Revisited." *Messenger*, November 1975:10-11.

34

A Small Town—with a Worldwide Reputation

Road builder Michael Danner and the Brethren pioneers of two hundred years ago would be thrilled to observe the small town of New Windsor still serving faithfully as the crossroad linking cities, countries, and continents to reach the needy with almost immediate relief.

Visitors from overseas arrive in the U.S. and are often amazed that the first people they meet have never heard of New Windsor, Maryland. When they finally locate the small town on a road map or find their way to the quiet village tucked away in the Maryland hills, they begin to understand why. How does it happen that a town with only a thousand residents has a worldwide reputation?

Here, on a former college campus at the edge of New Windsor, the Church of the Brethren operates the service center that is used by Church World Service, Lutheran World Relief, and many other world service agencies.

It's no wonder that visitors from overseas are surprised by the town's small size. They may have lived in

Europe in the harsh years after World War II, when food and clothing given by Americans came by way of New Windsor, bearing the name of the town on all the bales and packages. A daughter or son may have participated in an international youth exchange that began with orientation in the Maryland town. The medical supplies so important for a missionary doctor or nurse likely have reached their overseas recipients by way of a warehouse in New Windsor. The service center has been a temporary home for refugee families while they waited to be received in American communities. For many overseas artisans and crafters, the New Windsor address is the doorway to a market for their "self-help" products.

Most Americans don't expect New Windsor to be as conspicuous as Baltimore, but they, too, marvel that such a modest rural community welcomes around 35,000 visitors each year. Some come as volunteers to help in the humanitarian programs at the center, others as tourists attracted by its unique gift shop, and still others to participate in retreats.

No wonder the name New Windsor looms much larger in people's minds than on maps or road signs.

Morse, Kenneth I. *New Windsor Center.* New Windsor: Brethren Service Center, 1979.

35

A "Heifer Project"

One Sunday morning at the Oakland church in Gettysburg, Ohio, something unusual happened that set the stage for a memorable Thanksgiving service in 1972. Church member Beulah Maurer tells the story.

Our preacher, Fred Bernhard, told us that some weeks earlier he had awakened in the night with an idea. He woke his wife and shared his idea with her, gained her approval and support, and so decided to go ahead with it. That is *all* he shared with us, except for the admonition to "put your hands where your mouth is." He added that his idea would be revealed to all of us on the Sunday of our Thanksgiving celebration and dinner at church.

Maybe you can guess the speculation that went on. What kind of crazy scheme could Fred have in his head to be so mysterious about? Clever posters began appearing in the vestibule, one repeating Fred's slogan— "put your hands where your mouth is," another indicating the dates of the upcoming Sundays with a huge question mark after November 28.

As the day drew closer, there were some who began to guess much closer to the truth. Seeing the carpet covered with plastic on that Sunday morning confirmed the speculation. But none of us, in our wildest guesses, could have foretold just what was in store for our congregation.

After beginning worship and hearing Thanksgiving anthems by the choir, Fred reviewed the events of the past month, leading up to his "dream" for this Thanksgiving morning.

First, he borrowed a truck from a farmer in a neighboring congregation so that he would not have to reveal his reasons to any of our members. He made a quick trip in his truck to Somerset County in Pennsylvania, looked up some good friends with dairy herds of known quality, and shared his scheme with them. They offered their wholehearted support not only selling him stock at a very reasonable rate, but also donating some to the project.

At this point in the story, a door to the rostrum opened and out came four overall-clad farmers leading three little sweet-faced Holstein heifers. Eight more remained outside. Needless to say, the response was electric. All the children wanted to touch the animals—and they did.

Our pastor had acquired eleven registered heifers, ages two to six months, in the name of the Oakland congregation, acting only on faith and the belief that a true spirit of thanks-sharing would occur at our Thanksgiving celebration. He asked for donors and feeders. Slowly at first, then with growing enthusiasm, voices spoke out over the congregation: "This family will donate one," "I'll donate one and buy the feed if someone else will raise it," or "I'll go in with another family (or two or three) and raise one." Soon a line formed in the front of the church and one bewildered church clerk attempted to record all offers.

God moved in our midst at Oakland on that Thanksgiving. We felt him there and we all saw faith in action. When all the pledges were tallied up, there were enough pledges to buy *thirty-two* heifers.

It was Thanksgiving—and Fred didn't even preach a sermon—or maybe it was the best sermon he ever preached.

"A Thanksgiving Sampler from Richard N. Miller's Almanac." *Messenger*, Nov. 15, 1972: 16. Adapted.

36

A Lifelong Concern for Peace

As Charles Allen Smart traveled with his colleague John Baker to various parts of the world, he observed that on almost every occasion Baker quickly tired of tourist attractions, rather wanting to get into the streets and homes of poor people. Smart writes:

> Wherever he goes, to Cape Cod or the Congo, Washington or Bogota, he will wander around in a battered old hat, seeing and hearing everything, saying "Hello" to everyone and "Well . . ." to the hucksters, while thinking up and then actually realizing the most wonderful schemes for helping people to learn more and live better. . . .
>
> I liked the man at once; a rangy Pennsylvania farm type, skeptical but no cynic, zestful, and humorous but no sentimental gusher, and well aware of human pitfalls and sorrows. In time, of course, he grew on me, and he still does.
>
> He was obviously a very able man of the world, an operator, in fact, of the highest type not at all impressed by himself, and accepting as obvious the fact that organizing men, machines and money, with daring, imagination and tenacity, had one purpose

> only: the betterment of the conscious experience of individual boys and girls, men and women. With this conviction, it was inevitable that having been a businessman, he had become a professor, and finally the president of a university.

Now a centenarian at Brethren Village in Lancaster, Pennsylvania, Baker is a native of Everett, Pennsylvania. He was dean of the Harvard Business School and president of Ohio University, in Athens, Ohio. As a diplomat Baker was appointed in 1953 and again in 1955 and 1956 as chief United States representative to the United Nations Economic and Social Council (UNESCO) in Geneva, Switzerland. He later conducted state department studies of educational needs in Cambodia and Columbia.

In the mid-60s there were some questions on the part of Baker's American advisors as to the wisdom of making food supplies available to a Communist government—Yugoslavia. Baker simply said he liked and trusted their government's representative in the discussions.

Far more pertinent to understanding John Baker's concern for peace is his frequent quoting of a basic policy of the UNESCO constitution: "Since war begins in the minds of men, it is in the minds of men that the defenses of peace must be constructed. Nowhere is it more important to build these defenses than in the minds of college students." Baker also credits his wife Elizabeth for her eagerness to help men and women everywhere share in a world no longer dominated by conflict and violence.

To that end John and Elizabeth Baker have made generous contributions to peace studies programs on college and university campuses. On the basis of this strong peace conviction, they first established the Baker Peace Studies Fund at Juniata College in 1971.

Since 1993, international seminars in arms control have been conducted annually at the Juniata College Conference Center as a project of the U.N. Center for Disarmament Affairs and the International American Association of University Presidents. These seminars are supported financially by the Baker Peace Institute and directed by Andrew Murray, Juniata's director of Peace Studies. Selected scholars are given the opportunity to work together on disarmament problems and to build regional and international networks of people interested in arms control. The faculty for the seminars is composed of the U.N. experts, U.S. arms control policymakers, and leaders of international studies from various universities.

37

"Saint and Seer" in Peace Studies

Gladdys Muir (1895-1967), peace studies pioneer, was born into a loving family who nurtured her in many ways, including art and music. Although she was described as a shy person in her youth, she had inner strength and courage that drew her to teaching—a career that spanned fifty-two years at La Verne College (California) and then Manchester College (Indiana).

In 1947 Muir proposed that programs for the study of international conflict be established at each of the Brethren-related colleges. The Peace Studies Institute at Manchester College was the first program in the world to provide a major in peace studies and was a model for dozens of peace and conflict studies programs in the late 1960s.

Muir's zeal for peace was strengthened and encouraged by reading the great world philosophers. World War I also made a lasting impression on her and stimulated her interest in world affairs. During the summer of 1929 she traveled to Geneva, Switzerland, to learn more about the League of Nations and the next year to Scotland to study the British viewpoint on world questions. After attending the Institute of International

Relations in Whittier, California, sponsored by the Society of Friends, she accepted the validity of a religious approach to the war-peace question.

Muir was a demanding professor with high standards of scholarship for her students *and* herself. She exposed her students to "seers and saints," and with the depth of her knowledge, her classes became true educational feasts. She developed lasting friendships, inviting her students to her home for tea and discussion. She also wrote a bi-annual peace letter to almost three hundred students whom she considered as family.

Herbert Hogan recalls that "with her passing, the Church of the Brethren lost one of its greatest and most dedicated teachers, a creative, dynamic, humble seeker of the highest spiritual life."

Bulletin of the Peace Studies Institute. Manchester College, 1988 (anniversary issue).
Boyers, Karla. "Gladdys Muir: Peace Pioneer." *Messenger*, July 1991: 20-21.

38

Smeltzer in Selma: "A Faithful Soul"

A need for racial reconciliation and mediation in Selma, Alabama, became headlines in 1965 when Martin Luther King, Jr., made it the focal point in his campaign for voting rights legislation. Although Ralph Smeltzer (director of peace and social education for the Brethren Service Committee) had been working for a year in Selma to promote interracial peace and justice, the city was especially tense following the enactment of the Civil Rights Act of 1964.

There were some successes as Smeltzer tried to establish contact between black leaders and white leaders, but also times of discouraging failures. These failures came in talks with black leaders who were critical of other black leaders and among whites who were still forming plans to establish private clubs in a way that would make them immune from federal legislation.

Marie Foster, a black civil rights worker, describes a meeting she attended in Selma with Ralph Smeltzer and other civil rights activists. "After the meeting, Smeltzer felt like giving up, but he wanted to walk in the neighborhood and talk with people to see how they felt about recent developments. It was a dark, miserable night with steady rain and muddy streets, but talking with people as they sat on their front porches was a standard tactic used by organizers to plumb grass-roots attitudes. Smeltzer was prepared; he had on a raincoat and rubbers and . . . trudged through the rain into the night." Foster remembers thinking, "There goes a faithful soul."

Longenecker, Stephen L. *Selma's Peacemaker.* Philadelphia: Temple University Press, 1987.

The Widow and the General

—witness

39

"In Heart and Conscience Free": The Solingen Six

The price of freedom had been clearly stated. The six young men from Solingen, Germany, now imprisoned in the fortress at Jülich, could walk out any day they agreed to conform to one of the three tolerated religions: Lutheran, Reformed, or Catholic. So they were told by priest and pastors who tried to convince them of their errors. But they had been baptized as Brethren in 1714, and that was the beginning of their troubles, because such baptisms were illegal. Now they were under sentence for an indefinite term of hard labor, kept behind bars, threatened with torture, frequently interrogated.

They had been confronted by representatives of the Roman Catholic, Lutheran, and Reformed Churches. The Roman Catholics urged that they be executed; the Lutherans proposed that they be sent to the galleys; the Reformed, the most lenient, recommended hard labor at Jülich. On December 1, 1717, they were taken to the fortress and imprisoned there until their release on November 20, 1720. The six men were Johann Lobach, Wilhelm Knepper, Gottfried Luther Stetius, Johann Frederick Henckels, Jakob Grahe, and Wilhelm Grahe.

The fortress, in the form of a citadel, was once surrounded by a moat, with ramparts and thick walls. The men worked twelve hours a day in the moat—sometimes forty feet underground, sometimes on scaffolding on the tower. They lived in a dungeon several feet underground with walls ten feet thick. In their cells they made buttons by candlelight and sold them to supplement their poor diet. Occasionally they were trusted to work outside the walls.

The six young men responded with kindness to the ill treatment by their captors. They also wrote hymns and often sang when they could get together, and they had repeated visits from Brethren and Mennonites.

Wilhelm Grahe, who later married the daughter of John Naas, wrote a detailed account that was circulated widely among Pietists in Germany and Holland. He relates that "the people of Jülich were astonished that we had so many acquaintances and that we showed such love for each other." About their being tested, he writes, "We did not fear any man, because Jesus, his truth and teaching, were our protection and solace."

Durnbaugh, Donald F. "The Solingen Brethren." *Gospel Messenger*, May 3, 1958: 12-15.
Durnbaugh, Donald F. comp. *European Origins of the Brethren*. Elgin, Ill.: Brethren Press, 1958.

40

The Widow and the General

Ann Rowland deserves to be counted among the hundreds of courageous women who are not awed by generals. At the time of the Civil War, shortly before the battle of Gettysburg, General Robert E. Lee and his army crossed the Potomac in preparation for an invasion of Pennsylvania. They camped in Maryland, north of Hagerstown, near the Longmeadow church.

Among the Brethren families made anxious by the presence of the army was that of Ann Rowland, a widow with eight children. She tried to hide one horse when all her others were taken, but it was discovered and confiscated. The Brethren sister promptly went to General Lee, who was impressed with her courage and returned the horse.

But Ann Rowland faced the general on still another occasion, according to accounts remembered by her grandson. Lee had made his headquarters in the Longmeadow church. Ann was his first visitor. She came to ask him to turn over to her the pulpit Bible for safekeeping. The general refused, but he reportedly made this promise: "We used the Bible in morning worship. If it is left here, General Robert E. Lee pledges his honor that the Holy Word will be kept safely and no harm will come to this place of worship."

The general kept his promise.

Ankrum, Freeman. *Sidelights on Brethren History.* Elgin, Ill.: Brethren Press, 1962.
Henry, J. Maurice. *History of the Church of the Brethren in Maryland*, 1936.
Paul, Lois T. "Rowland, Ann Gilbert." *The Brethren Encyclopedia.* Philadelphia, Pa., and Oak Brook, Ill.: The Brethren Encyclopedia, Inc., 1983-84.

41

The Boys and Girls of the Highway

In February 1975, just a few months before his death, James Swallow, who had been an elder in the Church of the Brethren and the Dunkard Brethren Church, was interviewed by Kermon Thomasson. Seated in a rocking chair at his California home on Sonoma Mountain, the 91-year-old elder reminisced about his long life and described his recent ministry with young people.

You see, this love for the boys and girls of the highway, it sort of come through my evangelistic life. . . .

A young man came up here from San Francisco and he turned out to be an All-American football star with a university education. But he was just like setting somebody on fire. He was ready to go. At this moment he's in Hawaii, establishing a church there. . . .

We started what we call the Sonoma Light House Mission. [It] serves the boys and girls of the highways, the ones like I was, cast-offs, the ones that's down and out, got no place to go, no place to call home, nobody that cares for or loves them. They come here from everywhere now. If they want to get married they come. If they want to be saved they come. If they want somebody to listen to them they come. . . .

These boys and girls of the highway are coming in and laying their lives on the altar. I'm having a better time right now than I've ever had in my life. . . . Don't tell me that the Lord doesn't have a purpose for our lives. He does! He does!

Swallow, James, as told to Kermon Thomasson. "The Lord and Elder Swallow." *Messenger*, July 1975: 24-29.

42

A Study in Contrasts

Suppose Jesus had visited Brethren congregations in Pennsylvania around the middle of the nineteenth century. What would he have said about two preachers who were known to their families as Brother Jacob and Brother "Ashey"?

Brother Jacob was one of the first to preach in English in the vicinity where he served as a minister for about sixty years. He also traveled widely on preaching missions to other states, but he was probably most remarkable for his generosity to neighbors—even strangers—in need. A history of the church in his district gives details:

> A member of the Reformed Church, having lost a cow, came to Brother Jacob with a subscription paper. When he saw what it was, he tramped it under his foot, as he said, "Down in my barnyard are nineteen cows. Go down and take the best one, and say no more about it." Another asked to buy, on credit, a wagon Brother Jacob was not using. He said, "Take the wagon; there will be no bill. The scriptures teach, 'He that hath two coats, let him impart to him that hath none.' " In another instance,

when a neighbor's house burned, Brother Jacob bought the lumber and delivered it on the ground for a new house and refused any pay.

As for the other preacher, even his nickname tells about his attitude toward money. They called him Ashey because in winter, when roads were icy, rather than go to the expense of having his horses shod with winter shoes, he carried along ashes that he would spread on slippery spots.

At the end of the War of 1812, Ashey was in charge of paying off soldiers, so he arranged to get his pay in valuable tracts of land. Later, about the middle of the century, William Miller, the Adventist leader, persuaded many local farmers to sell their horses and cows because the Lord was coming and they would have no further need for them.

But when the second advent failed to meet their schedule, they asked Ashey, who had purchased cattle and horses from them, to sell back what had once been theirs. This he was willing to do—for a substantial profit. Now, as a man of property, Ashey was able to establish each of his six children on three hundred acres.

Middle Pennsylvania History, 1925.

43

How to Handle a Thief

One night John Herr was awakened in his farm home by the noise of robbers in his smokehouse. He found one thief standing at the door of the smokehouse to receive the hams that were handed to him by another thief on the inside. Although John Herr approached quietly, the thief on the outside was frightened and fled to safety without warning his colleague. The Brethren elder then took the thief's place at the door in order to receive the hams. The thief inside the smokehouse, who could not see Herr, asked how many they should take. Herr replied that they might as well take them all.

The thief inside, now aware that he had been trapped, started to run away, but the elder proposed that he take along a ham for his family. The thief refused, but Herr insisted and also reminded him, a neighbor whom he recognized, that if ever he was hungry he should not bother to come at night since he could have what he needed if he would simply ask.

John Herr never revealed the identity of the thieves. When they met him later, they could not look him in the eye.

The Brethren Encyclopedia. Philadelphia, Pa., and Oak Brook, Ill.: The Brethren Encyclopedia, Inc., 1983-84: 730 (sidebar).

Schlosser, Ralph W. "The Animated Preacher: John Herr." *Gospel Messenger,* Nov. 26, 1960: 14-15.

44

Peter Nead's Hat

Peter Nead, the man who so systematically defended the faith and practice of the Brethren, had to be guided, as a young preacher, into conformity with the Brethren manner of dress. John Smith, writing in the Brethren Family Almanac *in 1909, reveals how Benjamin Bowman tactfully brought the change about.*

Brother Nead's manner of dress was more stylish than Brethren custom. One feature of his attire that was particularly offensive to the Brethren was a tall white hat, often the style of the clergy in those days. Brother Nead was so earnest in his work and enjoyed his church relationship so much that fellow-Brethren were slow to ask him to put the hat away. Finally, old Brother Benjamin Bowman decided that he could remove that hat without offending Brother Nead.

One Sunday, after the close of the preaching services at his own house, Brother Bowman asked Brother Nead to take a walk with him. Entering the barn, he closed the door and took Nead to the far end of the floor, where he approached a fanning mill. Reaching into the mill, he drew out a new, low-crown hat and said, "Brother Peter, the Brethren feel that the hat you wear is not in harmony with the humble profession you have made. We love you and desire that you may do a great deal of good in the church. Now, Brother Peter, here is a new Brethren's hat that I bought for you." Holding the hat close to Brother Nead's face, he said, "Will you wear it?"

Brother Nead said, "Yes, I will." He took the hat and never wore any other kind of hat as long as he lived.

The kind manner in which Brother Bowman approached him had such an effect on him that he changed all his clothing and came in the full order of the church.

The Brethren Encyclopedia. Philadelphia, Pa., and Oak Brook, Ill.: The Brethren Encyclopedia, Inc., 1983-84: 404 (sidebar).

Smith, John. "Elder Peter Nead." *Brethren Family Almanac*, 1909.

45

The Stolen Ox

George Miller (1722–98) sought to live according to the gospel he preached. His grandson, who insisted he had the story on good authority, once recounted what happened when an ox was stolen from his grandfather. Miller, the first preacher in the Big Swatara (Pennsylvania) church, knew which neighbor stole his ox and where it had been taken. But it was his other neighbors, rather than he, who had the thief arrested and placed in the Lancaster, Pennsylvania, jail.

Miller felt sorry for the thief. He feared that his neighbor would be brought to the whipping post, as the law required. He was also concerned lest the thief have no bed when the weather was cold. So George Miller walked twenty miles to Lancaster to provide his errant neighbor with a bed in case he needed one.

The Brethren Encyclopedia. Philadelphia, Pa., and Oak Brook, Ill.: The Brethren Encyclopedia, Inc., 1983-84: 458 (sidebar).

Saylor, Guy, ed. *History of the Church of the Brethren in Eastern Pennsylvania, 1915-1965*, n.d.

46

The Generals Join in Family Worship

General George B. McClellan was an army commander during the Civil War, for a time the general-in-chief of the Union Army. In 1862, not long after the bloody battle at Antietam, which swirled around a Brethren meetinghouse, McClellan asked George and Mary Yourtee, who lived in a house that later served as a parsonage for the Brownsville, Maryland, congregation, to provide quarters for himself and members of his staff, including General Marcy and General Burnside. The Yourtees boarded the officers for several days during which the generals joined the family in their worship.

At this time Eli Yourtee, a young man in his twenties, was a likely prospect for the recruiting in which the generals were engaged. But General McClellan is reported to have encouraged Eli to become a minister, saying, "We need good young men in the ministry more than we need men in the army." Whatever McClellan's actual counsel may have been, Eli became an elder and leader among the German Baptist Brethren in the area.

For all his reputation as a general, McClellan may have been more in need of prayer at the Yourtee table than young Eli. McClellan's conduct of war following the battle of Antietam was "too cautious" to please President Lincoln, who soon relieved him of his command.

The Brethren Encyclopedia. Philadelphia, Pa., and Oak Brook, Ill.: The Brethren Encyclopedia, Inc., 1983-84: 475 (sidebar).
Henry, J. Maurice. *History of the Church of the Brethren in Maryland*, 1936.
Richard, W. S. "Death of Elder Eli Yourtee." *Gospel Messenger*, Oct. 9, 1909: 645.

47

John T. Lewis, Friend of Mark Twain

Mark Twain called him "the most picturesque of men" and "an implacable Dunker-Baptist." He was John T. Lewis, one of the few black members of the Brethren in the years before the Civil War, having united with the Pipe Creek church in Maryland in 1853, when he was eighteen years old.

Samuel L. Clemens (Mark Twain) had many reasons to admire Lewis, his friend for more than thirty years. Lewis had served as coachman for Clemens' father-in-law and later was a tenant farmer at Quarry Farm near Elmira, New York, where the famous writer spent many summers. On August 23, 1877, Lewis saved the lives of Clemens' sister-in-law Ida Langdon, her young daughter Julia, and a nurse, Nora, when a runaway horse dragged their carriage dangerously downhill toward a turn in the road. Clemens, in a letter to his friend William Dean Howells, describes how Lewis, who was coming up the hill with a load of manure, "gathered his vast strength and . . . seized the gray horse's bit as he plunged by and fetched him up standing!"

The rewards that John Lewis received for his courageous act enabled him to pay off his debts and also help his father, who still lived in Maryland. Writing a letter of thanks for the gifts he received, Lewis said, "Inasmuch as divine providence saw fit to use me as an instrument for the saving of those presshious lives, the honner conferd upon me was greater than the feat performed." That sentence, wrote Mark Twain, raised his letter to "the dignity of literature."

Of equal interest to Brethren is John Lewis's role in returning to the Antietam congregation in Maryland the large, leather-bound pulpit Bible that had been donated by the Daniel Miller family. The church, at the center of the battle of Antietam in 1862, was used as a hospital for the wounded. Eleven days after the battle, the Bible was taken by Sergeant Nathan Dykeman, who returned with it to Schuyler County, New York. When his regiment held a reunion in Elmira, New York, in 1903, the group decided to purchase the Bible from Dykeman's sister and return it to the church. Searching out a Brethren who could help them return the Bible, they located, of all people, John T. Lewis, who for many years was the only Brethren living in central New York. Lewis arranged for its return to Antietam forty-one years after its disappearance. The Bible is displayed periodically at the visitor center on the Antietam battlefield.

In preparing his own obituary, Lewis observed that though he had long been cut off geographically from the church, he had "tried to be faithful to the New Testament and order of the Brethren."

The Brethren Encyclopedia. Philadelphia, Pa., and Oak Brook, Ill.: The Brethren Encyclopedia, Inc., 1983-84: 851 (sidebar). Expanded.
Ankrum, Freeman. *Sidelights on Brethren History.* Elgin, Ill.: Brethren Press, 1962.
Henry, J. Maurice. *History of the Church of the Brethren in Maryland*, 1936.

48

Freedom—for Whom?

Freiheit ist uber Silber und Gold ("freedom surpasses silver and gold") is the noble sentiment displayed prominently over an arch in the city hall on the marketplace in Basel, Switzerland. Built in the sixteenth century, this city hall was familiar to Andreas Boni, one of the first eight members of the Brethren; its archives contain the record of his interrogation by the city's Council of Seven in 1706 regarding his Anabaptist beliefs.

Though better than silver and gold, freedom—or at least religious freedom—was not to be granted to Andreas Boni. First, he was expelled from the city. When he returned, he was imprisoned in the tower of the Spalen Gate at the west edge of the old city. From his prison, where he was placed for a time in the stocks, Boni addressed an open letter to the city fathers, calling on them and the city to repent:

> Now hear the words which God will give me to write, miserable creature that I am, through His goodness. I do not hesitate to write that this will be for the good of you, your city, and district of Basel. . . . With my clumsy hand I can hardly describe enough the sins and vices of this city. In sum, they all reach to

heaven. God intends to punish them if they do not turn to Him with all their heart.

Boni's open letter did not persuade the members of the council to repent, nor were they inclined to grant him religious liberty. Instead, they decided that "[h]e should be placed in the pillory, and again expelled forever under penalty of beating with switches."

The Brethren Encyclopedia. Philadelphia, Pa., and Oak Brook, Ill.: The Brethren Encyclopedia, Inc., 1983-84: 1010 (sidebar).

Durnbaugh, Donald F., comp. *European Origins of the Brethren*. Elgin, Ill.: Brethren Press, 1958.

49

John Naas—the Legend and the Reality

The John Naas story has been told so often that it seems to be more of a legend than an actual story. Although no documentation has yet been discovered, it is so consistent with records about John Naas that Brethren have been inclined to take it as part of their heritage.

John Naas lived in Krefeld, a part of Germany under the rule of the king of Prussia; therefore, it is logical that the Prussian ruler would have been eager to recruit men of strength and stature to be part of his bodyguard and to serve as members of his army—men like John Naas.

Telling of the following incident has been popularly received by Brethren for more than two hundred years: John Naas had been a minister in the Marienborn area of Germany until his family, along with other Brethren, were expelled and they settled in Krefeld. According to official records, Naas served there as elder of the congregation and traveled extensively in Germany and Switzerland, preaching, baptizing, and holding love feasts for the Brethren. The story goes that on one such journey, Naas was captured and tortured to force his enlistment in an elite regiment of the Prussian army. Naas refused, saying that he already had a captain, the Prince Immanuel.

Davis, Dorothy Brandt. *The Tall Man.* Elgin, Ill.: Brethren Press, 1963.
Durnbaugh, Donald F. "Naas, Johannes." *The Brethren Encyclopedia.* Philadelphia, Pa., and Oak Brook, Ill.: The Brethren Encyclopedia, Inc., 1983-84.

Krefeld (Crefeld) is an old town that did not thrive until the 1600s, about the time the Mennonites settled there early in the seventeenth century. Because of religious toleration, the community welcomed Mennonite refugees from other areas of Europe, who were among the early workers in the textile industries in Krefeld (silk, ribbons, linen, hosiery, etc.). In 1678 Mennonites were given citizenship by the Prince of Orange. Though they had a congregation, they did not build a church until 1695. Their church faces on Koenigstrasse, named after King William of Great Britain, Prince of Orange. The church was remodeled in 1843, partially destroyed in 1943, and rebuilt in 1950 with help from American Mennonites.

In the eighteenth century, Krefeld was under the king of Prussia. Since the king recognized the privileges of the Mennonite community, more refugees came there, including the Brethren, most of whom moved from the Marienborn area in 1715. Also, the Mennonite church was a refuge for Quakers and Moravians, as well as Brethren. The church had trained ministers who were friendly to the Brethren. Leaders of the church also intervened with government on behalf of people persecuted in Germany and Switzerland.

Johannes Brahms, the German composer, maintained close contact with Krefeld Mennonites from 1880 to 1897, especially the von der Leyen family (textile magnates) and von Beckarath families. The best-known drawing of Brahms at the piano is by Willy von Beckarath.

Peter Becker, Christian Liebe, and John Naas were among the leaders of the Brethren group between 1715 and 1719. They were not only active in Krefeld but also visited other cities in the Rhine area.

Durnbaugh, Donald F. "Krefeld." *The Brethren Encyclopedia*. Philadelphia, Pa., and Oak Brook, Ill.: The Brethren Encyclopedia, Inc., 1983-84.

50

A Dunkard and His Horse

Testimonies of the honesty and integrity of Brethren often come from unexpected sources, such as the Confederate officer who made wry comments regarding a Maryland farmer he encountered following the Civil War battle at Gettysburg.

Near Hagerstown I had an experience with an old Dunkard which gave me a high and lasting respect for the people with that faith. My scouts had a horse transaction with this old gentleman, and he came to see me about it. He made no complaint, but said it was his only horse, and as the scouts had told him, we had some hoof-sore horses we should have to leave behind. He came to ask if I would trade him one of those for his horse, as without one his crop would be lost.

I recognized the old man at once as a born gentleman in this delicate characterization of the transaction as a trade. I was anxious to make the trade as square as circumstances would permit. So I assented to his taking a foot-sore horse and offered him besides payment in Confederate money. This he respectfully but firmly declined. Considering how the recent battle had gone, I waived argument on the point of its value, but tried another suggestion. I told him we were in Maryland as the guests of the United States; that after our departure the government would pay all bills left behind; and that I would give him an order on the United States for the value of his horse and have it approved by General Longstreet. To my surprise he declined this also. I supposed then that he was simply ignorant of the bonanza in a claim against the Government, and I explained that; and, telling him that money was no object to us under the circumstances, I offered to include the value of his whole farm. He again said he wanted nothing but the foot-sore horse.

Still anxious that the war should not grind this poor fellow in his poverty, I suggested that he take two or three foot-sore horses which we would have to leave anyhow, when we marched. Then he said, "Well, sir, I am a Dunkard, and the rule of our church is an eye for an eye and a tooth for a tooth and a horse for a horse, and I can't break that rule."

I replied that the Lord, who made all horses, knew that a good horse was worth a dozen old battery scrub, and after some time I prevailed on him to take two by calling one of them a gift. But that night, about midnight, we were awakened by approaching hoofs and turned out expecting to receive some order. It was my old Dunkard leading one of his foot-sores. "Well, sir," he said, "you made it look all right to me today when you were talking; but after I went to bed tonight I got to thinking it all over, and I don't think I can explain it to the church, and I would rather not try." With that he tied old foot-sore to a fence and rode off abruptly.

Even at this late date, it is a relief to my conscience to tender to his sect this recognition of their integrity and honesty, in lieu of the extra horse which I vainly endeavored to throw into the trade. Their virtues should commend them to all financial institutions in search of incorruptible employees.

Battles and Leaders of the Civil War: The Tide Shifts, Vol. III. Edison, N.J.: Book Sales, Inc., 1985.

51

A Simple, Honest Man

Cyrus Bomberger was a farmer-preacher of the Spring Creek congregation in Lebanon County, Pennsylvania. He had a reputation as a man of unflinching integrity. When he took his wagon loads of wheat to Lebanon to be sold, the miller there told his workers that they need not examine the wheat, either to question its weight or check it for moisture, for Cyrus Bomberger was a man of his word.

In a song about Cyrus Bomberger, Andy Murray describes him as a "simple, honest man."

He's a full-measure man
He won't tell you a lie
When Cyrus rolls his wagons to the scales
Just wave him right on by
Level on the level, signed with the shake of a hand
Unaffected, well-connected
Simple, honest man.

The Brethren Encyclopedia. Philadelphia, Pa., and Oak Brook, Ill.: The Brethren Encyclopedia, Inc., 1983-84: 158 (sidebar).

Murray, Andy. "Granddaddy Was a Farmer." *Goodbye, Still Night,* 1978.

We Gather Together: Worship Resources for the Church of the Brethren. Elgin, Ill.: Brethren Press, 1979.

52

Good Neighbor Anna

While vacationing in eastern Pennsylvania, my wife Marjorie and I discovered we had two free days without any prior commitments. We turned to our hosts, the Earl Kurtzes and the Ross Noffsingers, for suggestions as to how to use this time best. Knowing of our interest in Brethren history, Amish ways, and new experiences, they glanced at each other for just a moment and said in unison, "Anna Buckwalter."

In a few moments, they had Anna on the phone. Our excursion to historic places in Lancaster County would include wholesome food at Amish/Mennonite restaurants, an introduction to her Amish neighbors, and a commercial bus tour on the second morning, with Anna herself in charge.

Described as an "Ambassador of Good Will," Anna met us on the first day at a restaurant near Lancaster with plans to visit Amish homes in her own neighborhood. She was especially eager for me, an editor, to meet the editor of an Amish magazine that was edited, printed, and mailed from one large farmhouse, using power sources other than electricity. That weekly

Amish paper included church news concerning meetings still held in homes and personal items about members. We were surprised with a short ride in an Amish buggy pulled by two prancing horses and driven by two young Amish women employed by the Amish magazine editor.

We also stopped at the historic Hans Herr House, the restored home of one of the earliest Mennonite settlers in Pennsylvania. We then visited the Lancaster Mennonite Historical Society which has the finest collection of material on Mennonite and Brethren families in this country.

The next day our bus ride with Anna began at a hotel in downtown Lancaster. For the next three hours, Anna, who was dressed in plain Brethren garb, pointed out places of interest in Lancaster. After a stop at a pretzel factory, she introduced us to the Amish people as we drove slowly past their fields and their homes. She also included a stop at an Amish/Mennonite-owned craft shop near Strasburg.

Since the newspaper editor had not been at home when we stopped the first day, we were invited back the following evening. As we sat in the family room of the big house, the setting sun slowly disappeared, and the coal oil lamps were lighted one by one. It was just the way we remembered the coming of dark in farm homes before they had electricity.

When Anna entertains visitors, she makes a point of informing them firsthand about family life, farming, and other aspects of the Amish community without actually disturbing them. She says, "In their own simple way the Amish have what the whole world would like to have: peace, prosperity, security, and strong families."

Anna still lives in a refurbished school house that she and her husband, John, who died a few years ago, made into a home in 1938. For more than fifty years, Anna and her husband continued their good neighbor ministry from this home. They hosted students from countries around the world who were attending nearby Lincoln University. They also provided taxi service for the Amish when they needed help in getting farm equipment delivered or when an Amish woman needed to get to the hospital in time for her baby's birth. Their home was also the headquarters for a program that placed hundreds of city children in country homes by means of a Summer Fresh Air Fund.

Columnist George Will writes of Anna's neighborly deeds: "She's a plump mountain of good will from her prayer covering to her feet." He also says, "She does this from her kitchen in Ronks with a telephone that rings off the hook and beneath a wall sign which says, 'Seven Days Without Prayer Makes One Weak.' "

53

"Are You Saved?"—"Ask My Neighbor"

The extent of Rufus P. Bucher's evangelistic work is impressive—more than two hundred series of meetings resulting in almost three thousand accessions to the church. On his return from one such meeting, Bucher encountered a young stranger in a railway depot who handed him a tract entitled "Brother, Are You Saved?" When the young man put that same question to Bucher, the Church of the Brethren farmer-preacher replied, "That is a good question and deserves an answer. I think, however, that I might be prejudiced in my own behalf. You better go down to Quarryville [Pennsylvania] and ask George Hensel, the hardware merchant, what he thinks about it. Or you might go to the Mechanic Grove grocer or to one of my neighbors in Unicorn. While there, you might ask my wife and children. I'll be ready to let their answers stand as my own."

The Brethren Encyclopedia. Philadelphia, Pa., and Oak Brook, Ill.: The Brethren Encyclopedia, Inc., 1983-84: 461 (sidebar).

Saylor, Guy, ed. *History of the Church of the Brethren, Eastern Pennsylvania, 1915-1965*, n.d.

"This *Is* West, Madame"

—migration

54

Intermarriage

The course of true love seldom runs smoothly; and there is potential for trouble when one lover or the other, or perhaps both of them, belongs to a sectarian group. If the couple comes from two separate denominational backgrounds, or if they discover they have quite different religious leanings, they face decisions that can create tension in the home and even in the church.

In 1717, only a few years after the Brethren movement was launched at Schwarzenau, Germany, a young minister in the Krefeld congregation, who had been baptized a Brethren but who occasionally preached for the Mennonites, fell in love with a Mennonite woman named Eva op den Graef. His name was Wilhelm Hacker. The young girl's stepfather, a Mennonite minister who later joined the Brethren, performed the marriage ceremony. But several people in the Krefeld Brethren group opposed any marriage with people outside their fold. They voted to excommunicate Wilhelm, but others in the congregation wanted only to suspend him from membership for a time.

Hacker, though supported by his wife and father-in-law and befriended by many Brethren, was so troubled that he fell sick and died. The damage to the congregation was serious because it produced a split in the church. It may even have prompted the migration of many members in 1719 to the American colonies. One observer noted that at least one hundred people who were ready to join the Brethren drew away because of the divisive spirit in the church.

When Andrew Snowberger (1744-1825) and Barbara Karper were married in Pennsylvania, they were both Brethren. But then Barbara met Conrad Beissel, the leader of the Ephrata movement, at a love feast, and she decided she would join the Seventh-Day German Baptists whom Beissel led. In a compromise respecting their differences, the couple agreed that she would worship on Saturday and he would continue to worship on Sunday in the Brethren fashion. But tensions remained.

One day Barbara, accompanied by their small child, left home and began the long walk to Ephrata. Andrew followed, caught up with her, and agreed to join the

Seventh-Day people if she would return so that their family could be united.

The Andrew Snowberger home was the first meeting-place for the Snow Hill colony that started near Waynesboro, Pennsylvania, in 1798. Andrew was the first prior for the community, a spin-off of the Ephrata cloisters that continued there through most of the nineteenth century.

In 1800 Jacob Early, who had recently emigrated from Germany, married Magdalena Wenger, the daughter of the Mennonite farmer for whom he had gone to work near Harrisonburg, Virginia. Though the young couple was in love, they could not agree about church affiliation. Jacob, who was Lutheran, respected the Mennonites but refused to become a member. Magdalena was just as adamant that she could never become Lutheran. They took their predicament to John Flory, a Brethren elder, who knew how to resolve the problem. Flory invited them to become Brethren and later baptized them. They had eight children, the youngest of whom was Noah Early, the father of H. C. Early, who served eight times as the moderator of Annual Meeting. Most of the Earlys of Virginia are descended from the Lutheran husband and Mennonite wife who settled their differences by becoming Brethren.

Wright, Lee-Lani, ed. *Church of the Brethren Handbook on Church Unity*. Elgin, Ill.: Brethren Press, 1988.

55

Westward into Conestoga Country

Members of the Church of the Brethren began to arrive in America in the early 1700s and were organized on Christmas Day in 1723 in Germantown, Pennsylvania.

As missionary zeal bloomed among the new members in the Schuylkill Valley in "the Conestoga country," organized mission efforts were formed. One such missionary party out of Germantown organized itself into two groups—one party going on horseback and the other on foot. The party on horseback followed the road and arrived in the Conestoga Valley (then part of Chester County) on November 9, 1724. They stayed all night at the home of Jacob Weber near Weberstown, Leacock Township. The party on foot took a shorter route over the Welsh Mountains and spent the night at the home of Hans Graeff. This was in Earl Township, at a site now known as Groffdale.

Both parties met on November 10, 1724, at the home of Hans Rudolph Nagele, a Mennonite preacher. The groups spent the night at Stephen Galliond's and the next day retraced their steps and journeyed toward the Valley of the Pequea.

On Thursday, November 12, a meeting was conducted at the home of Heinrich Hohns. At this meeting, seven people applied for baptism and were immediately baptized in the Pequea by Peter Becker. This was the beginning of the German Baptist Brethren in Lancaster County.

Gleim, Elmer Q. *Brethren Beginnings in Lancaster County, Pennsylvania,* n.d.

56

West and South by the Monocacy Road

Michael Danner, a German immigrant who later became Brethren, acquired land west of the Susquehanna River and was one of five Pennsylvania commissioners appointed in 1744 to open up highways for use by eighteenth-century travelers as they made their way from the Susquehanna to Frederick, Maryland. Today the communities along these roads are served primarily by routes 116 and 30.

Elmer Q. Gleim, author of *Change and Challenge*, a history of the Southern District of Pennsylvania, points out significant places along this route.

Columbia (Wright's Ferry on the Susquehanna River)

In 1738 this community, once an Indian settlement, was founded by John Wright. It was later considered as a possible capital of the U.S. Many Brethren pioneers crossed the river here on their way to new homes farther west and in Maryland and Virginia. The commissioners carved a rough trail through the wilderness beyond the Susquehanna (1739–1741) and named it for the Maryland river to which it brought travelers. The Monocacy Road was actually an extension of the Conestoga Road (1733) which bore traffic from Philadelphia.

East Prospect

Michael Danner and other Brethren first came to this region in 1728. They were forcibly removed from their earliest settlement, and he was imprisoned in Maryland, because he refused to acknowledge himself a tenant of Lord Baltimore. This was all part of the border dispute that resulted in establishment of the Mason and Dixon line in 1767.

York

York became the seat of government for "the United States" (Sept. 30, 1777–June 27, 1778) under the Articles of Confederation.

East Berlin

Clement Studebaker, who arrived in America in 1736, settled along Beaver Creek east of East Berlin. David Studebaker, a minister of the German Baptists, owned a home in the community. His home has since become a museum open to visitors. Clement Studebaker was listed as a house carpenter in the year 1799. He was the forerunner of the family that produced the wagon and the automobile.

The Brethren Home and Cross Keys Village (intersection of routes 30 and 94)

An old inn, constructed in 1869 for travelers between Philadelphia and Pittsburgh, was purchased by Brethren in 1951 and developed into a retirement village and campus with several buildings. District offices are located here.

Mason and Dixon Line (separating Pennsylvania and Maryland)

Charles Mason and Jeremiah Dixon settled a century-old border dispute in their survey made 1763–1767. This line runs close to Black Rock Church of the Brethren.

Bermudian Church

The congregation was formed by families who had moved from Amwell, New Jersey, in the 1750s to an area where there were also many followers of Conrad Beissel (Ephrata Cloisters). In the early years, services were held in homes and in a store before the church was built in 1856.

Gettysburg (Routes 15 and 30)

Recognized nationwide for its association with the Civil War battle July 1–3, 1863, the community has many historical sites, including the national cemetery, the setting for Lincoln's Gettysburg Address. A number of Brethren families in the Marsh Creek congregation were impoverished by the battle. Members of Codorous and Pipe Creek congregations sent relief in the form of clothing, blankets, food, and money.

Gleim, Elmer Q. "A Brethren Travel Guide for Southern Pennsylvania" (pamphlet), n.d.

57

Hazards in the New World

In July 1755, during the wheat harvest in a fertile valley near Blacksburg, Virginia, Shawnee Indians captured Mary Ingles, a farmer's wife, and took her with them to a Shawnee settlement in Ohio. Mary was purchased by Indian hunters who took her to Kentucky. Escaping into the forest, she found her way back to Ohio, Kanawa, and New Rivers until in mid-winter she arrived home to be reunited with her family.

Although Mary Ingles likely was not Brethren, her family was closely associated with German Baptists, both from the Ephrata group and the Germantown group who lived on the frontier. Her story, based on records kept by early settlers, is the subject of a popular novel, *Follow the River*, by James Alexander Thom.

Flory, Rolland F. *Lest We Forget and Tales of Yesteryears*, Vol. 1, 1973.

Margaret Replogle, a girl of fifteen, was seized by American Indians in 1766 while attending a husking bee near her home in Bedford County, Pennsylvania. Margaret dropped patches from her handkerchief and apron along the way, but her trail was lost, and she lived with her captors for seven years. They then sold her to the French who turned her over to the English at Detroit where she was set free. She walked all the way back to her Pennsylvania home, where her parents had almost lost hope of seeing her again.

Hanawalt, Pearl. *Hahnewald* (privately printed history of the Hanawalt family), 1961.

At the 1922 Annual Meeting, M. G. Brumbaugh told the story of "Sawquehanna, the White Lily," the name given by American Indians to a Martin family child who was captured during the French and Indian War. She soon forgot her native language and grew up as an American Indian. Sixteen years later, the girl was one of 125 white children released from captivity and returned to Pennsylvania where they hoped to find their families. Among those seeking word of their children was Sawquehanna's mother. Unable to recognize her daughter in any other way, she sang a Pennsylvania German melody that the girl remembered. In this manner they were reunited.

Beckner, W. O. "Sawquehanna, the White Lily." *Gospel Messenger*, 1922: 484.

58

"This *Is* West, Madame"

According to Reuel Pritchett, his ancestor Jacob Bowman was the first Dunker to migrate from Virginia to Tennessee.

The first Dunker who ever attempted to live on Tennessee soil was Jacob Bowman, father of all the Tennessee tribe of Bowmans. He was my great-great-grandfather. Brethren were migrating from Pennsylvania down to Maryland and from Maryland down into Virginia. Jacob and his wife, Susana Millhouse Bowman, settled first in Rockbridge County, Virginia, where the Natural Bridge is now. Susana was born in Germany, and German was Jacob's native tongue.

The couple was caught in the fever to go west through Tennessee. As handed down in several lines of the family, the story has it that in about 1782, Jake and Susana left their seven children behind and headed west with two horses and a Conestoga wagon. With them they had oats, corn, fodder, flour, meal, a side of meat, a rifle gun, a chopping axe, tin plates, a bone-handled knife, a two-pronged table fork, quilts, a change of clothes, and their German Bible. They forded Little River, they forded New

River, they forded two or three prongs of the Holston River—there were no bridges—and in the Tennessee wilderness they forded the Watauga River.

As they curved along Sinking Creek in Carter County, they spotted a couple boiling molasses. They stopped, fed the horses, tied them to the high wagon wheels. Jake Bowman strolled down to the creek, talked with the folks, and bought some molasses. After molasses for supper, with enough left over for breakfast, they read their Bible and prayed for their children back in Virginia. Then, spreading the quilts over the fodder in the covered wagon, they retired for the night.

As the sun filtered brightly through the forest, Susana called out, "Jake, it's daylight."

"Yeunnnh." He was soon snoring again.

After a while she jobbed him and said, "Jake, I tell ye it's daylight. Ain't ye gonna feed the horses?"

"Yeunh, I'm gonna feed 'em." Over and back to sleep he rolled.

Susana poked him a little harder and said, "Jake, I thought we was goin' west."

"This is west, madame," he says.

They finally got up from the fodder, had a hearty breakfast of molasses and side meat, and fed the horses. They looked around, and Jake made a purchase contract for a piece of land right there on Sinking Creek in Carter

County, a little east of where Johnson City is now. Then they headed back to Virginia to get the children. But Jake sickened with typhoid fever and died in Rockbridge County. Susana Millhouse Bowman, brave woman that she was, took the younger five of their seven children and started west again in that Conestoga wagon.

Joseph Bowman, the eldest of the children who accompanied her, became a deacon and a prominent man among the Dunkers. He married the young widow Hoss, built a splendid big colonial brick house and raised a family. When the Hoss woman died, he purchased a mile square of land on Knob Creek in Washington County and married Christena Beam. He raised another big family of children, out of which has issued maybe forty preachers or more. My mother came through that medium. I'm a great-grandson.

In 1818 Deacon Joseph Bowman built a masterful big brick house in the shape of an L on this mile square, and the whole house was two-story, all of it. The partitions on the first floor were removable, and that's where the Knob Creek Brethren had church until 1834 when they built a log church-house chinked and daubed on a corner of his farm. That's the church-house I grew up in.

Pritchett, Reuel B., with Dale Aukerman. *On the Ground Floor of Heaven*. Elgin, Ill.: Brethren Press, 1962. Adapted.

59

Westward on the Ohio River

According to family tradition, the George Wolfe family was used to rugged adventure, since they had thirteen years earlier moved 250 miles by four-horse wagon over the Alleghenies to Fayette County, Pennsylvania. The elder Wolfe was an industrious, hard-working German who had managed to accumulate property and was both a farmer and a boat builder. By the year 1800, transportation by boat on the Ohio River was heavy; the elder Wolfe and his two boys, Jacob and George II, rushed the work on their boat so they could start by early April in 1800.

At the start, the course was north, then west, past the present city of Pittsburgh, and then north and west until the Ohio River was reached. The speed of the boat was regulated largely by the swiftness of the stream. There were other boats on the river, many going and some returning. . . .

The downstream journey was considered easy enough, but to bring a loaded boat from New Orleans up to any of the points along the upper Ohio was a laborious task, often requiring months. At the end of the down trips, the boats were often sold and the lumber in them utilized in constructing buildings. In building their boat, the Wolfe family probably had this in view. On reaching their destination, they would have lumber enough to erect a fairly comfortable farm building.

We are not advised of the number of persons occupying the boat. It may have been of sufficient size to accommodate another family or two, at least there were in all likelihood other men besides the elder and his two sons. These would have been a help in handling the boat in the spring when the waters were high and the current swift.

Day after day the boat wended its way southward and westward as flowed the great Ohio River between Ohio and what is now known as West Virginia. There were no cities to grace the banks on either side. Here and there, miles apart, a small village, just a few houses, might be seen. One great almost unbroken forest lined the stream for hundreds of miles. . . .

In the passing woodlands were plenty of deer, wild turkey, and other game. An hour on shore with the unerring aim of the rifle of either Jacob or George might easily have meant enough venison or wild turkey for the better part of the week or longer. With a bit of fishing tackle, an ample supply of the best of fish at any time was an easy and sometimes an exciting proposition. At one end of the boat, probably the stern, was a low log pen, say five feet square, filled with earth to the depth of eighteen inches, and lined with stone around the edges. Over a blazing fire on this temporary hearth, the mother hung her cooking pots, and here she, assisted by her daughter or daughters, prepared the daily meals, and baked the corn pones to satisfy the craving appetites of the active crew that manned the floating vessel that was her home, her kitchen, her dining room, parlor, and sleeping apartments all combined. Or, she may, on leaving her Pennsylvania home, have insisted on taking on board her nice cooking stove, and with that properly installed, she could have done her cooking with more ease and comfort.

. . . Such trips, however fascinating, were not without their dangers. Here and there were roving bands of Indians, some wild animals, the panther, the bear, and wildcat. Not a few boats were constructed with boarded up sides, behind which men could shelter themselves in self-defense, when fired upon from the shore. The Wolf [as the craft was named] was not likely thus equipped, for Elder Wolfe had found that he could get along with the Indians by treating them kindly. Still, Tige [the dog] was on deck all hours of the night, and though his eyes might be closed, his ears, dog-like, never slept. A bit of noise, so faint as not to reach the human ear, causing a low growl from Tige, would quickly bring the young men from their bunks ready for an emergency.

. . . So far navigation had been attended with little danger, but on reaching the point opposite where Louisville now stands, 130 miles from Cincinnati, the whole family realized that they faced a serious proposition, one dreaded by all those doing business on the river. Here the river has a drop of twenty-six feet in two miles, a wonderfully swift current for large flat boats. For the Wolfe boat, it meant every man at his post with poles, sweeps, and steering paddle to keep the floating craft rightly headed in the rushing current. To safely steer a well-loaded boat through these rapids for two miles was no child's play. It required nerve, skill, and strength, but the father as well as the young men were brave, almost daring, and performed the feat with perfect safety to the great relief of the nervous mother.

Another hundred miles and they were where Green River enters the Ohio from the Kentucky side. Now began the real tug of war, for with sweeps, poles, and even ropes handled from the shore, the boat must be worked upstream. This called for strength, patience, and physical endurance. The destination of the family was Logan County in the southern part of the state and meant a river trip of at least sixty miles and then twenty or more miles by land. But just how far the boat was taken is not known. As there was a great demand for well-made river flat boats, the father may have sold it and then conveyed his goods by wagon across the country. At any rate, we soon find Elder Wolfe and his family at the end of their long journey, permanently located, some historians say, in Muhlenberg County, while others have the place of residence in Logan County. The evidence seems to be pretty well balanced, but we are inclined towards the latter.

Elder Wolfe doubtless purchased a farm and settled down to business. He was a well-to-do man and could afford to have about him the necessary farming conveniences of the times. Having his two sons with him meant farming results a little in advance of the ordinary. While the elder was industrious and enterprising, he was also deeply interested in the work of the church he represented.

Moore, J. H. *Some Brethren Pathfinders*. Elgin, Ill.: Brethren Publishing House, 1929.

60

Westward by Railway

Many Brethren were involved in railway migration, moving their families and all their possessions to western states, taking advantage of land offers well publicized in Brethren publications shortly after the turn of the century.

Magazines, such as *Gospel Messenger*, *The Inglenook* and *The Brethren Family Almanac,* that came to Brethren farm homes carried full-page advertisements paid for by railway companies and their agents, bearing testimonials from Brethren who had already gone west by rail and now were able to tell about their financial success and the churches they helped to plant.

The agents represented such railways as the Great Northern Railway, the Northern Pacific, and the Santa Fe, not only in advertising but in special promotional activities at Annual Meetings, often with the assistance of ministers who were employed by agents. After several years the Annual Meeting limited the railroad companies to sales outside the grounds, but some of the more aggressive agents continued to attend the conference so they could work individually on their prospects.

Preaching in a Tavern

One of the most graphic stories of Brethren moving their families west tells of a special train planned entirely for taking emigrating families from northern Indiana to North Dakota in 1894. The movement had assumed large proportions and a colony of Brethren in North Dakota was definitely assured.

Aided at every opportunity by a general immigration agent, Max Bass, the Reverend A. B. Peters traveled from community to community in the midwest, telling farmers of the wonderful opportunities that awaited them in the northwest. He visited the homes of those he thought he could interest, took a meal with them, or perhaps stayed overnight. And because he himself was a poor man in a new country, the people he approached placed confidence in him. In the smaller towns, public meetings were called for the purpose of informing large numbers of people about North Dakota.

By 1894 a new church and cemetery had been built in Zion, North Dakota, and stories of the church activities were circulating in great detail among Indiana farmers who were considering moving to the northwest.

For families already well established in communities around Walkerton and Nappanee, Indiana, leaving their homes and moving with all their children and their farm equipment in wintertime would be a traumatic experience under the best of conditions. But for the particular group of Brethren who left Indiana in March 1894, there were other elements to discourage less venturesome people. Brethren, coming mostly from farms and small towns in Marshall and Elkhart Counties in Indiana, brought their families and household goods, livestock, farm machinery, in fact everything. Those who owned land either sold it or offered it for sale. They prepared to sever all connections with their old homes and to establish themselves permanently in new ones.

A special train was to make the trip to Cando. March 27 was the date set for departure. For several days prior to this date, Walkerton was the scene of unusual activity. Everybody was busy loading household goods and livestock into freight cars. The excitement caused by their leaving for a new state was accelerated by the leave-taking of friends and relatives. Rumors of the terrible hardships to be met in North Dakota, the rigor of its winters, were on every tongue.

In addition to the stories of starving and freezing, news of the Bomberger murder had just reached Indiana, and friends of the colonists freely predicted for them a similar fate. It seems that in July of 1893 the Daniel Kreider family (the mother, father, and four of the children) had been massacred by their cousin Albert Bomberger, who was living with them. The father had asked the young man to leave because he did not approve of the attention the young man was paying to the nineteen-year-old daughter (who survived the tragedy). Bomberger was tried in Cando and hanged.

Despite the news from North Dakota, the colonists were not deterred. They continued their preparations for leaving and found that comradeship in a new and uncertain venture made new friends, so that their sorrow at leaving was not wholly without recompense. The gathering of such a large number of people and their effects naturally caused some delay, and it was not until two o'clock on the morning of March 28 that the long train was ready to start.

That special train in the spring of 1894 was just the first.

Miller, G. Edwin. *The Life and Genealogy of David Y. Miller.* Privately printed, 1989. Adapted.

61

Northwest Bound

Howard Michael was almost too small to remember the dangers and excitement of traveling more than two thousand miles from the sod house his family left in the western plains to the territory of Washington, along the Pacific coast. During a four-and-a-half-month trip by wagon train, the Michaels were joined by other Brethren families.

We visited Uncle Ben Michael's a few days in Dundee County, Nebraska; but over two thousand miles beckoned to us, so on June 6, 1889, we made an early start westward.

Peter Michael, my father, a proficient blacksmith and carriage maker, had made metal brackets which held a one-by-twelve-inch plank horizontally on either side of the wagon bed. Those supported the bows for the cover and gave an overall width of 6 feet 4 inches. A bed spring and mattress were then placed crosswise at the rear of the wagon, giving storage space by day and a sleeping space for some by night. He also fitted the oxen with horse collars turned upside-down, then used a harness which gave the oxen more freedom for walking than the yoke had done.

Preaching in a Tavern

. . . As we neared Denver, moving objects were seen far ahead and our telescope showed them to be wagons. We urged our oxen to their fastest walk and by nightfall overtook a five-wagon caravan. They were Oregon-bound and we were welcomed by them. After replenishing our provisions in Denver, a passing cowboy agreed to show us through Denver and put us on the right road into the Rockies; and a nice cash thank you was made up for him.

Higher and higher we climbed, eventually reaching snow-line at Berthoud Pass; and there, just below the melting snow, were beautiful lilies blooming. Nearing Idaho Springs, Colorado, mother had a high temperature. In a nice area we all camped where in walking distance could be seen a nice ranch home. Father went to inquire if there was a doctor in the town. Mrs. Anderson, matron in the home, replied, "There is none"; but a lady visiting in the home spoke up, saying, "I am a registered nurse and will gladly go and see if there is anything I can do." Graciously she went to the wagon and found that all symptoms indicated Spotted Fever, but her kit held the remedy. At her insistence she took our baby sister to her home to care for until mother could convalesce.

. . . After mother's fever broke, she and father went to the home and gave our benefactors all they would accept—

many heartfelt thanks. The caravan then moved out, with mother improved but as yet with no appetite. At a rushing stream, father caught a lone trout, which she relished; then she began showing greater improvement.

. . . We camped one night in Bago, Wyoming, and later another wagon arrived with J. D. Freeman, his wife, and baby; and they were welcomed into our group. Bago folk urged us to take the Cherokee Trail, saying the Laramie Route was badly rutted by recent great droves of cattle.

Three days later we camped on the bank of Shell Creek, the site of a recent round-up, for the branding irons were still there. In the morning all wagons moved out with none imagining impending tragedy. Only a few miles out, we crossed a shallow ash, and there in sand moistened by a summer shower were large bear tracks. Mr. Freeman called all the men and said, "Here are fresh bear tracks, my dog says so. Let's hunt him down for camp meat." All camped in open spots in the sage. Mr. Freeman's dog, which had treed several bear back in North Carolina, hunted for a while, then in midday heat refused to try. Mr. Freeman then followed the tracks, while Mr. Barnett and father hunted about gunshot range on either side. About a mile further on, the old grizzly had found a dense bunch of sage, circled out and came back almost to his starting place, and there he bedded down where he could watch the back trail.

As Mr. Freeman passed his lair, the bear sprang, knocking the 45-70 Sharpe rifle from his hands and knocking the man down. A fourteen-year-old boy, unarmed, had followed Mr. Freeman, and his wild yelling alerted Mr. Barnett and father and they came running, but neither could get a shot. Mr. Freeman's lungs were pierced, air was wheezing out. Father, heavily muscled and of 220 weight, picked him up to carry to the wagons. The victim whispered that he could not endure the pain. The other men ran to bring the wagons and Mrs. Freeman, while father bared the wounds and held them closed so that his breathing might be easier. Mrs. Freeman arrived in time to hear a few words before he died. After partially recovering her composure, she sobbed, "What can my baby and I do now?" Father voiced the mind of all in his reply, "Rest assured you will share with the rest of us." Mrs. Freeman, an orphan, and now a widow, and not yet twenty years of age, had yet another problem, for only ten dollars remained in their treasury.

. . . The wagons moved slowly away and few words were spoken that day; but in the evening two cowboys rode up and asked of the trip. A brief account was given of the fateful hunt, and after a pause, one of the cowboys asked if shortness of provisions had prompted the hunt. Assured that it had, they rode off but soon were back leading a fine fat calf. One dismounted and with a six-shooter in hand asked where it should be killed. When that was accomplished they rode off, probably never realizing how much new courage their willingness to become involved had brought to a heavy-hearted, short-provisioned group.

Months of helpful fellowship, dangers, and tragedy had made strong friendships; but Boise, Idaho, was the point of sad farewells. The Barnetts [and others in our train] left on the Malheur Route for Southern Oregon, while we planned to take the Burnt River Route toward Washington.

Our family and Mrs. Freeman made camp near a farm close to Boise. The owner, a fine gentleman, came out and assured us that we were welcome to what fruit we could use from his orchard and to make jells if we chose. And what a treat that was! The farmer also helped father find sale for Mrs. Freeman's oxen and wagon. He located an elderly couple who would give her and her child a home and a dollar per week to do their housework. Boise had been the Freeman destination; so with the little sum for her outfit and a place to live, she started life anew. Again there were sad farewells!

We had admired the grandeur of the Rockies, were entranced by the change from sage brush to the Blue Mountains of Oregon, but we were totally unprepared for the breathtaking beauty that greeted us as we climbed into the Cascades of Washington. . . . At Snoqualmie Pass we stood in awe of the rugged snow-capped peaks which seemed so close. When we started down the old switchback, zig-zag road, down the steep bluff to the Snoqualmie River, we found it a hard one to descend safely, but we finally made it.

Through rains and muddy roads we drove into Seattle several days later and camped in the area of the present Georgetown District of Seattle on October 16, 1889, the end of the four-and-a-half-month camping trip. Father walked across to a market where a huge pile of freshly caught salmon was on display and asked the price. The answer was "Two bits." He handed over the twenty-five cents and carried to camp a nice large salmon and said, "Let's celebrate for we are at our destination, Seattle, Washington Territory!"

Personal accounts of Howard and Elsie Michael. Brethren Historical Library and Archives, Elgin, Illinois.

It was an unlikely spot for a church that would continue over a hundred years. But Coquille Valley in southwestern Oregon was the isolated area picked by three Brethren families who left Iowa in 1872 looking for a homestead on the Pacific slope. The church that the Barklow family organized a year later (Coquille Valley congregation, later Myrtle Point) began almost immediately to reach out for new members. By 1894 the congregation was serving twelve different preaching points in the valley.

The adventurous faith of such pioneer Brethren is evident in a letter the Barklows sent to the Christian Family Companion *(Jan. 14, 1873):*

After twelve days' travel, we arrived within twenty miles of the place where we wished to settle, and the way would not admit a wagon any farther. . . . There we remained for three days, while we prepared one-horse sleds, suitable to pass on a trail, by which we conveyed our goods through a dense forest of fir and cedar, over a small mountain, cutting our way through, and bridging logs by throwing smaller logs against them, so that a beast could pass over. In this way we worked through to the Coquelle River, the distance of eight miles . . . . After being here a short time, we notified the people that there would be preaching in the grove a short distance from our houses, on the coming Sabbath, where there assembled a good and attentive congregation . . . . We think, the Lord willing, churches will spring up in Oregon.

The Brethren Encyclopedia. Philadelphia, Pa., and Oak Brook, Ill.: The Brethren Encyclopedia, Inc., 1983-84: 295 (sidebar).

Eller, Vernard. "Key 73/Coquille 1873." *Messenger,* May 1973: 30-31.

Muir, Gladdys. *Settlement of the Brethren on the Pacific Slope.* Elgin, Ill.: Brethren Publishing House, 1939.

62

Friendly and Not So Friendly Debates

Around 1817, just before Illinois was admitted to the U.S. federal union as a free state, George Wolfe II and a Baptist minister named Jones held a joint series of revival meetings in the southern Illinois community where Wolfe had resided for several years and where a Brethren congregation was established. Even though this was a time when denominational differences were vigorously debated, the two preachers remained on friendly terms while defending the practices of their respective denominations. At the conclusion of the meetings Wolfe and Jones shook hands.

Thirty-three years later, when Union County (where the meetings had taken place) decided to adopt a seal, the engraver pictured two preachers facing each other and shaking hands. Some have suggested that the name chosen for the county in 1818 reflected the spirit of union manifested by pioneer ministers like Wolfe and Jones. But the name might also have been chosen because 1818 was the year that Illinois was admitted to the federal union.

The Brethren Encyclopedia. Philadelphia, Pa., and Oak Brook, Ill.: The Brethren Encyclopedia, Inc., 1983-84: 1358 (sidebar).

The atmosphere was not nearly so friendly on another occasion when George Wolfe, II, was challenged to debate a Roman Catholic priest at Kaskaskia, the first capital of Illinois. Religious issues were intensely regarded then (around 1820) and Kaskaskia was already a stronghold for Catholicism. So skillfully and forcibly did our pioneer preacher meet his opponent at every point that after the discussion was over the governor of the new state, Shadrach Bond, who presided at the debate, arranged for a military escort to accompany Wolfe on his way home.

Moore, J. H. *Some Brethren Pathfinders.* Elgin, Ill.: Brethren Publishing House, 1929.

Throughout the nineteenth century, Brethren were frequently involved in public debates on religious issues. Leaders such as Isham Gibson (1830s), D. B. Sturges (1840s), John Kline (1850s), James Quinter (1860s), R. H. Miller, and S. H. Bashor (1870s and 1880s), among others, defended Brethren ordinances and beliefs in debates with representatives of other denominations. Often the sharpest debates were with groups that had much in common with Brethren but who differed in their form of baptism or their observance of the Lord's Supper. Debates lasted from one day to a week and often drew crowds of more than a thousand people. Arguments were based on Bible texts and church history. Out of such debates there developed a body of literature, including books, tracts, and a series of magazine articles, that helped to define the distinctive practices of the Brethren.

Martin, Dennis D. "Debates." *The Brethren Encyclopedia.* Philadelphia, Pa., and Oak Brook, Ill.: The Brethren Encyclopedia, Inc., 1983-84.

63

Scruples of Conscience

Peter Cartwright (1785-1872) was a famous Methodist preacher who traveled widely in Kentucky and Tennessee and other frontier states. In Illinois, he was twice elected to the state legislature. His Autobiography *tells of an argument in the legislature between Cartwright and a lawyer from Union County whose constituents included several congregations of Brethren. Cartwright's comments about the encounter were quite critical of the Dunkers.*

This lawyer represented that they kept Saturday for the Christian Sabbath, and thought, or professed to think, it was altogether wrong that they should pay taxes, work on roads, perform military duty, or serve on juries, . . .

He wanted to have a law passed, favoring them in all these particulars, and thus exclusively legislating for their particular benefit, thereby making a religious test, and making a sectarian distinction, and legislating for their pretended scruples of conscience. He accordingly introduced a bill for their special benefit. I opposed the passage of the bill, and briefly remarked, that as a nation, we all acknowledge Sunday as the Christian Sabbath, and that there ought to be no distinction in Churches, or among the people; and as to bearing arms, that the people who were unwilling to take up arms in the defense of their country, were unworthy of the protection of government. . . . The representative from Union . . . began to eulogize the Dunkers and drew a contrast between them and the Methodists. He said the Dunkers were an honest, industrious, hard-working people; their preachers worked for their own support; there was no hypocritical begging among them; no carrying the hat around in the congregation and hypocritical whining among them for support, as was to be seen among Methodist preachers.

The Brethren Encyclopedia. Philadelphia, Pa., and Oak Brook, Ill.: The Brethren Encyclopedia, Inc., 1983-84: 647 (sidebar).

Cartwright, Peter. *Autobiography.* Nashville: Abingdon, 1956.

64
The Garden of Eden in Ohio

Could the Garden of Eden, the home of Adam and Eve, have been located in Ohio? A Brethren minister thought so. Indeed, Landon West was ready to offer a number of reasons why the ancient paradise must have centered around Great Serpent Mound in Adams County in his native state.

West's theory differed markedly from the notions of archeologists who visited Serpent Mound after it was first surveyed in 1849. The mound is about one thousand feet long, in the form of a serpent whose bent body and curled tail extend along a hilltop. The serpent's jaws are opened wide as if ready to devour an oval-shaped object.

West believed that the mound was created by the hand of God as a lesson to the world, that its forms were symbols of Satan and of the forbidden fruit with which the serpent tempted Eve. The minister quoted Job 26:13 (KJV): "By his spirit he hath garnished the heavens; his hand hath formed the crooked serpent."

West is reported to have said, "This figure is the most ancient record of history known to exist. It shows first sin and its immediate results as Moses also records them. . . . [It] supports the written or inspired history of the human race."

According to archeologists, Serpent Mound is one of many "effigy" mounds built by American Indians around one thousand years ago. Some were used for burial purposes; others may have been intended for religious rituals.

The Brethren Encyclopedia. Philadelphia, Pa., and Oak Brook, Ill.: The Brethren Encyclopedia, Inc., 1983-84: 1332 (sidebar).

Randall, E. O. "Ohio, the Site of the Garden of Eden." *Ohio Archeological and Historical Publications*, Vol. X, 1901-02: 225-231.

65

The Johnstown Floods

Brethren were among the settlers who came to the Johnstown, Pennsylvania, area before the town was chartered in 1800. And Brethren were directly affected by the three disastrous floods that swept through the city in 1889, 1936, and 1977.

One Brethren woman, Nannie Hanawalt Strayer (1863-1955), had vivid memories of those tragic days in May 1889.

I was in the living room and noticed a rush of water with wood. As I looked, I saw people on parts of houses. I went to the rear and looked out of the bathroom window. All small buildings were swimming. I called to the men to come quickly; all the houses around us were floating away . . . .

The houses on the other side of the street were all gone. The brick ones melted away. We thought our house would stand. Suddenly it was struck. The plaster came down. The front windows were broken. Water was rushing in upon us. Papa saw a hole and some light and climbed out; took Clarence [her four-year-old son] up and then helped me get out on the driftwood. . . . We were sailing with the wreckage, but did not know we were moving. Fourteen people were on our roof. . . . A man . . . got another to help and they pulled us up onto the roof . . . .

The men of our party went down and helped to arrange a path that we could crawl out. All bridges were gone and our only way out was toward Green Hill. . . . Clarence and I were getting along very well, I thought. A man with two children came and took Clarence on his back . . . .

We did no weeping until we came to a battered tin roof on which fourteen dead people were placed. . . . A great crowd of people was gathered, waiting and watching for their friends. I felt ashamed to shed tears when we came to them. They had Clarence in their arms. They asked him where Papa and Mama were. He said, "They are coming." They knew that we were alive.

In July 1977, eleven inches of rain descended on Johnstown in a six-hour period. Once again several Brethren families suffered the loss of property and loved ones. Three members of the Walnut Grove congregation were among the one hundred people in the city who lost their lives. The Mack Religious Bookstore, operated by the Church of the Brethren in downtown Johnstown, suffered great loss and was not reopened. Several church buildings belonging to various Brethren groups were moderately damaged.

In this instance the church-at-large was better prepared than in 1889 to respond quickly with offers of aid. The Brethren Disaster Network, with coordinators at work in most districts, responded to an appeal for help from the local disaster center in the Walnut Grove church. Within a few weeks, more than 6,500 volunteers were put to work in "mudding out," cleaning up, or repairing buildings and distributing food and clothing.

The Brethren Encyclopedia. Philadelphia, Pa., and Oak Brook, Ill.: The Brethren Encyclopedia, Inc., 1983-84: 673 (sidebar).

Hanawalt, Pearl. *Hahnewald (Hanawalt)*, privately printed history of the Hanawalt family, 1961.

Bohrer, Wendell. *Johnstown, A Story of Tragedy and Love*. Elgin, Ill.: Brethren Press, 1978.

66

The Ecumenical Meetinghouse

The first Brethren in America were opposed to erecting buildings for congregational worship, choosing to gather in homes and occasionally using a barn for love feasts. When they did decide to build, they insisted that the structure be simple and plain, without pulpit or altar, without steeple or bells, without any ornament or decoration. They placed ministers and elders on the same level with other worshipers, thus affirming the priesthood of all believers.

Annual Meeting ruled that meetinghouses be used only for worship and for ordinances such as the love feast, and not rented or offered to other groups except for funerals. Yet there are scattered records of meetinghouses being used jointly with other denominations.

In York County, Pennsylvania, the Altland house began as a log structure used in the late 1700s by German Lutherans and Reformed Calvinists, as well as by German Baptist Brethren. It was replaced by the present brick structure in 1853 that provided space for all three groups. A union Sunday school continued until 1906. The youth of the Bermudian Church of the

Brethren sparked a project to restore the historic meetinghouse in time for its re-dedication in 1981.

Three miles south of Easton, Maryland, a large historical marker, erected by the Maryland Historical Society, catches the attention of travelers on Route 50. Any who stop to read the plaque will learn that the unique six-sided building nearby is the Peachblossom Meetinghouse. Built in 1880 by members of four faiths—Brethren, Lutheran, Methodist, and Swedenborgian—the odd-shaped building was used by each denomination every fourth Sunday.

After a few years, Brethren continued to use the building regularly, but others less frequently. It was called the Peachblossom Meetinghouse because the first peach trees in Maryland were planted nearby. Brethren, who became sole owners of the property, continued to use the building for worship until 1902 when they purchased a building in Easton.

Through the years, the building was left to deteriorate until 1971, when Gilbert Walbridge, a builder in the Easton congregation, took charge of restoration. After ten years' work, it was re-dedicated on the occasion of the congregation's 100th anniversary.

Because the traditional meetinghouse emphasizes simplicity, offers flexibility, and encourages participation by the entire worshiping community, many of its values have been incorporated into church buildings used currently by Christians of many denominations.

Wright, Lee-Lani, ed. *Church of the Brethren Handbook on Church Unity.* Elgin, Ill.: Brethren Press, 1988.

67

Paradise Prairie: The Monument of a Dream

It had the most promising name for any congregation in the Southwest, but that did not guarantee a long life. The Paradise Prairie congregation in Oklahoma was started in 1892 with twenty members. For many years it prospered, reaching a membership of more than eighty and counting among its active young people a future meteorologist of world renown (Harvey H. Nininger) and an educator and writer (Cecil B. Williams), who would tell its story in the novel entitled *Paradise Prairie*. But as early as the 1920s it was evident that emigration would reduce its membership. In 1963 the Paradise Prairie congregation ceased to exist.

Cecil Williams writes of the people and community that nurtured his youth: "Whatever the soul of America is . . . it has got to be what has been created through the lives of men like my father, and through the dreams of people like those who established the Paradise Prairie Church of the Brethren. It's not a story of success so much as a story of stumbling and falling and getting up again, always aspiring."

Of the dream of the early settlers who started the church he writes, "The name of Paradise Prairie was the monument of a dream more than anything else, but it had been a significant dream."

The Brethren Encyclopedia. Philadelphia, Pa., and Oak Brook, Ill.: The Brethren Encyclopedia, Inc., 1983-84: 993 (sidebar).

The Hayloft Reporters

—Annual Conference

68

A Gloomy and Dreadful Time

In 1856, when the first Annual Meeting in the "far west" was held near Lena, Illinois, Pentecost came early. It was cold, it rained each day, the mud was ankle-deep, the host farmer broke his arm, and his wife was ill. Reporting in the July issue of The Gospel Visitor *that year, Henry Kurtz described the weather as "another trial of the faith."*

Towards Lord's day evening the heavens lowered, and soon after night a thunderstorm arose with heavy rain, and from that night on till Wednesday morning or nearly noon scarcely the sun was seen, and more or less rain almost incessantly poured down. Besides, the air became so damp and chilly that those who had no overcoats suffered from cold.

This was indeed a gloomy and dreadful time for such a meeting. The rich, black soil by constant rain was so softened, and by moving to and fro of so many people so much tramped and loosened, that every vestige of grass disappeared and one step from the door a person would sink in the mud ankle deep, while the rain continued to pour down. It was impossible for people coming in the house to clean their shoes sufficiently, and so the mud was carried into the house upstairs and everywhere in such quantities that it became difficult to walk up and down stairs without slipping. I never saw a house in such a condition before.

69

The Brethren Connection

Traveling by horseback in 1846, young Abraham Harley Cassel took almost a week for a roundabout journey from his home to the Annual Meeting at Royer's farm in Lancaster County, Pennsylvania. There were stops overnight near Reading and Lititz and Mount Joy (where he "conversed until nearly 3 o'clock in the morning") and at Elizabethtown. Almost every meal was taken at a Brethren home; and there were frequent gatherings at homes, in barns, and in a schoolhouse, where Brethren from Maryland and Virginia shared their words of testimony with their Pennsylvania hosts. Including the days he participated in the Annual Meeting, Cassel observed that he was absent from home for thirteen days and traveled about two hundred miles.

In 1855 Brethren decided to locate Annual Meetings in places accessible to railroads. *The Gospel Visitor* had already carried information about train schedules.

Some railroads built special spur lines or sidings for the convenience of rail travelers. Special reduced fares were offered. Excursion trains were provided just for Brethren. One traveler wrote enthusiastically about cars "overflowing with Brethren," providing opportunities for "interchange of greetings" and "the formation of new acquaintances." But sometimes other transportation was needed to carry the delegates from the train to the conference. In 1870 Iowa Brethren met the train with an ox cart since there were "no regular roads" on the prairie. In 1871 a young delegate told how he was "perched high upon the top of an old-fashioned wood and leather, spring, four-horse stage coach," where he enjoyed "a fine view of the magnificent country."

At the close of the 1893 Annual Meeting at Muncie, Indiana, an elderly brother, John Metzger, led devotions at the end of the meeting, saying, "We have had an enjoyable meeting. To me it was a feast and I will not forget this meeting till I go to my grave. Sixty-three years ago I traveled through this neighborhood and lodged in the timber here. It rained nearly all night and there was no shelter near where Muncie is now. At that time ravenous beasts and savages were to be seen. Now we are highly favored, brethren and sisters in the Lord, in that God's people can meet here and worship Him in His appointed way."

"Sidelights on Brethren Annual Meetings." Prepared by the Brethren Historical Committee for Annual Conference at Norfolk, Virginia, 1986.

70

Pentecostal Preaching

In 1846, at John Royer's farm near Lancaster, Pennsylvania, Annual Meeting preaching services began on Sunday morning at 7 and continued until 12:30 in the afternoon without intermission. While the congregation sat on rough boards without backs, twenty bearded Brethren ministers preached, one after the other, for an average time of fifteen minutes each. Among the preachers there were George Hoke, John Kline, Peter Nead, Henry Kurtz, James Quinter, and Adam Brown.

Because of the crowds that attended Pentecost Sunday services at Annual Meetings, preaching services were sometimes scheduled for several locations. In 1865, at Franklin Grove, Illinois, two editors preached simultaneously in a large tent—Henry Kurtz at the north end, preaching in German, and James Quinter at the south end, preaching in English.

One young man at the 1905 Annual Meeting in Bristol, Indiana, was impressed with the preaching of I. N. H. Beahm, who spoke about light and darkness during a thunderstorm. As Brother Beahm was describing the light of the gospel, lightning flashed. When he referred to the darkness of the world, the lights of the auditorium went out. When he again mentioned light, the lights came on.

"Sidelights on Brethren Annual Meetings." Prepared by the Brethren Historical Committee for Annual Conference at Norfolk, Virginia, 1986.

71

Annual Meeting in Wartime

Despite the unsettled conditions of a nation divided by war, Annual Meeting was held in Virginia in May 1861. David Miller of Lima, Ohio, was one of the handful of northerners in attendance. He noted a spirit of union and love and order in the meeting attended mostly by Virginians. Facing delays but no serious difficulties in traveling from Ohio to Virginia, Miller wrote, "There was no danger, or at least we saw none. Some of the soldiers at Harpers Ferry said they looked with eager eyes to see the Brethren go through. . . . A captain . . . said that such people as we could travel in the South where we please."

The officers of the meeting, fearing that mail would be stopped, arranged for a Maryland brother to take the records of the meeting to a Pennsylvania brother near the boundary line, who mailed them to the editors of the *The Gospel Visitor*.

"Sidelights on Brethren Annual Meetings." Prepared by the Brethren Historical Committee for Annual Conference at Norfolk, Virginia, 1986.

72

Feeding the Five Thousand

Five thousand people, including the governor of Pennsylvania and his secretary of state, came for Sunday dinner at the Annual Meeting of 1866. The people of the Antietam (Pennsylvania) congregation were well prepared, having started months ahead of the conference to procure food and supplies. They built a tent 190 feet by 90 feet for dining and a smaller tent for cooking. They hired a local butcher to kill the beef, render the tallow, put hides in tanners, and to deliver the meat. Food supplies included flour (3,200 lbs.), beef (8,000 lbs.), sugar (120 lbs.), coffee (230 lbs.), bread (13,000 lbs.), pickles, and ham. Apple butter brought in crocks was to "be submitted to the committee to judge quality." A brother was allowed to sell pies and bread, but "no strong drinks." And feed for horses was also available.

Imagine the quantities of food required as attendance at Annual Meetings reached surprising proportions, especially during the later 1800s and the early 1900s. Although some estimates of attendance, especially on Pentecost Sunday, seem overblown, the figures are remarkable for a small denomination of an estimated 50,000–60,000 members at that time.[1] As early as 1846, it was reported that between two and three thousand members participated in the Conference love feast.

One way of gauging relative attendance at early Annual Meetings is to note how much food was needed for the gathering. D. H. Fahrney, a local historian in the Antietam congregation compared the provisions of four Annual Meetings that his church hosted. In 1810 one sheep provided enough meat; in 1829 it took one ox; in 1847, four or five oxen; and in 1866, fourteen or fifteen steers.

1. *The Brethren Encyclopedia,* Vol. III (Philadelphia, and Oak Brook: The Brethren Encyclopedia, Inc., 1984) 1475.

"Sidelights on Brethren Annual Meetings." Prepared by the Brethren Historical Committee for Annual Conference at Norfolk, Virginia, 1986.

73
The Hayloft Reporters

In 1873 Henry B. Brumbaugh was the editor of *The Pilgrim*, one of the four main church periodicals published by the Brethren at that time. He knew that most of his readers wanted reports of speeches at the Annual Meeting (held in a barn at Meyersdale, Pennsylvania, that year), but he was aware that the church was not quite ready to accept full reporting at that meeting. He wrote later:

> Our decision was in favor of the report and we planned to get it in a way that would cause no disturbance in the meeting. So we employed our reporter . . . and located him on the hayloft directly over the floor where the meeting was held. It was not as desirable a position as our reporters now get, but it was good enough to get a fairly satisfactory report. The interesting feature of the occasion was that Brother H. R. Holsinger, of the *Christian Family Companion,* also had a reporter for his paper and brought him to the hayloft. Though competitors, we, personally, were on good terms and united our efforts in getting as good a report as possible.

The Annual Meeting that year was still inclined to restrict reports, ruling that a synopsis of reasons leading up to a decision could be given but no names of speakers were to be included. Holsinger insisted, however, in publishing the names in the next year's report. Brumbaugh tried to help his readers by numbering each speaker and printing a separate "key" that would give the names for each number. He said, "The demand for the key proved as great as [the demand] was for the report." Both editors were called to account, but a year later the Annual Meeting decided in favor of a full report.

The Brethren Encyclopedia. Philadelphia, Pa., and Oak Brook, Ill.: The Brethren Encyclopedia, Inc., 1983-84: 1069 (sidebar).

Brumbaugh, Henry B. "Forty Years in the Chair." *Gospel Messenger*, 1910: 89-90.

"Sidelights on Brethren Annual Meetings." Prepared by the Brethren Historical Committee for Annual Conference at Norfolk, Virginia, 1986.

74

A Taste for Color

The Annual Meeting of 1877 was held in New Enterprise, Pennsylvania, in a large barn belonging to Obadiah Over. The stone building that now houses New Enterprise Church of the Brethren stands at the same location. At one point during the sessions, a report was circulated that the floor of the building was giving way. The report was unfounded, and the meeting continued.

In another issue, while holding to rigid dress requirements for men (standing collar was reaffirmed as the old order) and for women ("sisters should not wear any hats at all"), the meeting heard J. H. Moore argue for a little color in hymn books. He said, "The Lord himself had a taste for different colors when he made you and me; he wanted some with black hair and some with red, and some with auburn to suit his taste. Some of us have blue eyes, some black, some grey—and making flowers he put different colors in them—hence I see no impropriety in using different colors on our hymn books, provided they are plain."

"Sidelights on Brethren Annual Meetings." Prepared by the Brethren Historical Committee for Annual Conference at Norfolk, Virginia, 1986.

75

A Memorial Service Long Remembered

Although James Quinter had wide appeal as a preacher, was known for his success as a debater and his support of higher education, was influential in church publishing, and served as editor of Gospel Messenger, *the manner of his death is almost always mentioned first in connection with his name.*

His colleagues D. L. Miller and H. B. Brumbaugh give firsthand accounts of the 1888 Annual Conference in North Manchester, Indiana.

We come now to describe a scene of peculiar and touching sadness, one that time will not soon efface from our memory; . . . We refer to the death of our dear aged brother, Elder James Quinter. He reached the meeting-grounds about noon on Saturday and greeted a number of those he loved so well, for all who knew him loved him, and this general feeling of love and respect shown him was fully reciprocated in his great sympathetic heart. He expressed himself as not feeling so well, and it was generally observed that he did not seem as strong as usual.

At 3 P.M., Brother Daniel Vaniman preached in the Tabernacle, and Brother Quinter left the *Messenger* office, saying he would go and hear the sermon. It was to be the last he would hear in this world. He closed the meeting with the words of the following hymn, which he read in a most feeling and touching manner.

In the beginning was the word, across the
  chaos night;
It gleamed with quick creative power, and
  there was life and light.
Thy word, O God, is living yet amid earth's
  restless strife,
New harmony creating still, and ever higher
  life.

And as that word moves surely on, the light's
  resplendent ray
Streams farther out across the dark, and night
  grows into day.
O word that broke the stillness first, sound on
  and never cease
Till all earth's darkness be made light, and all
  her discord peace;

Till wail of woe and clank of chain, and battle
  noise are stilled,
And all the world, O God of love, with harmony is filled;

Till selfish passion, strife and wrong thy summons shall have heard,
And thy creation be complete, O Thou Eternal Word.

The text of this hymn appears in *The Brethren Hymnal* (1951) with a tune written by Donald Frederick and entitled "James Quinter."

Quinter then spoke a few fitting words upon the sermon to which he had just listened, and kneeling in prayer he thanked God that he was once more permitted to meet with those of like precious faith. It was noticed by those near him that his voice trembled, but the words were clear and coherent, and as he said "We are glad to meet again," his voice ceased, never more to be heard in this world. Those who were kneeling by his side noticed that he grew very pale. Saving arms held him from falling to the floor, and he was tenderly and gently raised from his knees and laid on the table. He gasped a few times, and then, surrounded by a weeping congregation, his spirit took its homeward flight. And so passed away one of our great and good men, not great as the world counts greatness, but great in all the noble qualities of true Christian manhood. "We are glad to meet again" were his last words, and as he uttered them his voice was hushed in death. Were these words spoken of us, or were they spoken to those on the other shore who were watching and waiting for the coming of our dear brother? God only knows.

After it was known that Brother Quinter was dead, the Standing Committee adjourned its session and proceeded in a body to the Tabernacle, where his body was lying. Brother Enoch Eby made a few appropriate and touching remarks to the weeping congregation. A prayer was then offered and the remains were taken away and prepared to be taken to his former home in Huntingdon, Pennsylvania.

—D. L. Miller

Henry B. Brumbaugh describes Quinter's death in a similar way, noting the enthusiastic greetings that he received from the Conference when he arrived and that he took some moments of rest at the Conference office. On hearing Brother Quinter had died, Brumbaugh notes that "the scene of his death, there in the midst of the loved and the loving, we shall not attempt to describe. It was sad—so sad, and yet so glorious—so glorious! It was a death so near not being a death, that it seemed befitting to say, 'Brother Quinter is not dead—God has taken him.' "

It fell to Henry Brumbaugh and his brother to make the arrangements. Quinter died at 4 P.M. and by 9 P.M. the arrangements were complete.

What Brumbaugh did not report was the confusion at Huntingdon when Quinter's fellow-church members received the wire: "The body will arrive at a [given time]." Either the Brumbaugh brothers assumed the Huntingdon church members would automatically know it was James Quinter who had died, since he had complained of not feeling well a few days before the Conference, or they were exhibiting Brethren thrift (the message would have cost more with each added word). It is more likely that the Brumbaughs were involved in caring for so many details that they could not think of everything. In any case, Henry Brumbaugh reported a record attendance at the memorial service held at Huntingdon, with seventeen ministers taking part in the service.

On a tree-shaded sidewalk near the Peabody Retirement Home in North Manchester, there is a bronze plaque marking the exact spot where Quinter died.

Quinter, Mary N. *Life and Sermons of Elder James Quinter*, 2nd ed. Elgin, Ill.: Brethren Publishing House, 1909.

76

Suspicious Characters

Brethren attending annual meetings were often the victims of pickpockets. Reuel Pritchett describes the situation at the 1905 Conference he attended at Bristol, Tennessee.

A number of our sisters staying at a certain rooming house began missing a few of their effects. They got to suspicioning a particular person dressed in the garb but who maybe wasn't a sister. Then more effects disappeared along with the suspicioned person. They got to figuring out that it wasn't even a woman but a man dressed like a sister. That caused quite a sensation among the sisters and Brethren.

Pritchett, Reuel, with Dale Aukerman. *On the Ground Floor of Heaven*. Elgin, Ill.: Brethren Press, 1980.

"Sidelights on Brethren Annual Meetings." Prepared by the Brethren Historical Committee for Annual Conference at Norfolk, Virginia, 1986.

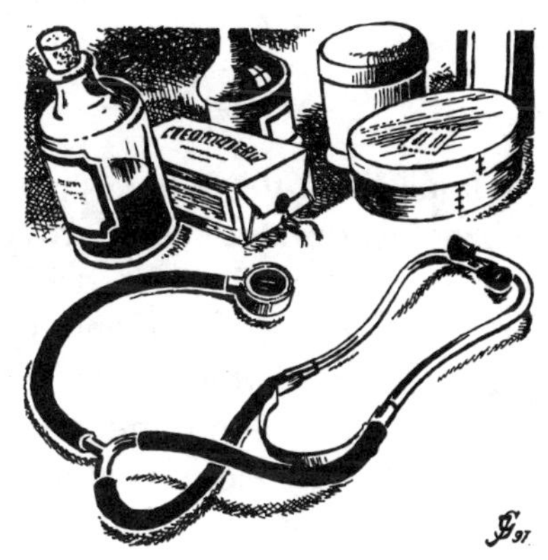

The "Hen Medics"

—vocation

77
An Editor's Viewpoint

As familiar as Alexander Mack must have been with the village of Schwarzenau, Germany, he could easily have lost his way in the crowd of several hundred people who congregated there on August 6, 1958, for the 250th anniversary of the beginning of the Brethren movement. Not that Schwarzenau had changed much in 250 years. Many buildings appeared much as they did in 1708. And the Eder River moved just as complacently along its serpentine path.

But the wave that swept over the village on the day of the anniversary was largely a human wave. People came in buses and cars, and many who lived nearby walked the short distance to the school yard where a large tent had been erected. Of the several hundred people there, more than half were Europeans who were not Brethren but who had had contact with recent Brethren activities in Europe.

As a member of the Church of the Brethren delegation, I had looked forward eagerly to my first visit to Europe and the opportunity to visit historic places, learn about Brethren programs, and file my news reports and editorial comments for the *Gospel Messenger.*

Naively, I had assumed that the occasion would bring together a small gathering of Brethren, mostly from the United States, who could celebrate the anniversary while a few local citizens looked on. But I soon discovered that the people of Schwarzenau, together with other Europeans who had hosted exchange students or received heifers or in some manner come in touch with Brethren workers, regarded this as their anniversary also.

As the day progressed, I began to understand how a Brethren anniversary of the birth of a sectarian movement could become an ecumenical event. One of the speakers, Dr. W. A. Visser 't Hooft, then general secretary of the World Council of Churches, noted that the spiritual descendants of those who were forced by their convictions to separate themselves from eighteenth-century churches were now participating fully in the fellowship of churches around the world.

Visser 't Hooft offered two reasons for this remarkable change. First, the Brethren had become less a sect and more like other churches. Inevitably, this represented some loss in the intensity of their spiritual experience, but it also indicated a growth in responsibility. Second, the changes in the established churches, from which the Brethren had separated, were even more profound. These changes occurred, he said, largely because of the contribution of groups like the Pietists and Brethren, whose influence he called "the unfreezing of a frozen church situation." Revival of personal religion, emphasis on practical Christianity, the subsequent missionary movement—all these helped to "unfreeze" and reform the churches.

The service of worship at the convocation indicated how Christians from widely differing backgrounds could share in praise and celebration despite language and custom barriers. Hymns, such as "Fairest Lord Jesus," "A Mighty Fortress," and "Praise to the Lord, the Almighty," were sung by German and English worshipers concurrently in their own languages, with a little stumbling, but with blended voices and great mutual satisfaction.

Morse, Kenneth I. "After 250 Years." *Gospel Messenger*, Sept. 20, 1958: 14-19.

Wright, Lee-Lani, ed. *Church of the Brethren Handbook on Church Unity*. Elgin, Ill.: Brethren Press, 1988.

78

Around the World Without a Cent

Many people dream of traveling around the world. Although some make it, few are as daring as Henry M. Spickler, a graduate of Mt. Morris College, who in 1901 was challenged to circle the globe by ship and by bicycle. The bicycle was provided by a local newspaper in Polo, Illinois, in exchange for letters from Spickler describing his trip.

Having no other resources, Spickler wrote: "I am the man who rode a bicycle around the world without a cent. On leaving school in the year 19—, I passed out of the east door of our home in Polo, Illinois, kissed my mother and sister good-bye, and without a single penny in my pocket, with my face to the east, resolved to keep going until I rode around the earth and entered our home by its west door."

It took Spickler three years to cover forty thousand miles and visit twenty countries before he could greet his mother at the west door. He worked at seventy-five different occupations to cover his expenses, which ran about five to ten cents a day. He was arrested in France, locked up in Germany, and lived with brigands in the Holy Land. In India he visited Wilbur Stover, a fellow student at Mt. Morris, who had gone there a few years earlier.

Spickler wrote descriptive articles for his hometown paper and for the *Mt. Morris Index.* Brethren readers followed his adventures in the pages of the *Inglenook* in 1908 and 1909, and the book he wrote and published in 1922, *Around the World Without a Cent*, was widely distributed. Spickler, who once stumped the state of Illinois for prohibition and helped in D. L. Moody's crusades, was also in great demand as a speaker on the Chautauqua and lyceum circuits.

The Brethren Encyclopedia. Philadelphia, Pa., and Oak Brook, Ill.: The Brethren Encyclopedia, Inc., 1983-84: 1273 (sidebar).
Spickler, Henry M. *Around the World Without a Cent.* n.p., 1922.

79

Not in the Number of Words

In the 1870s two similar Brethren publications were competing for the same reader. When the publishers of *The Brethren at Work* asserted that their paper in its enlarged form would be the largest in the brotherhood, an elder in Iowa set out to correct the statement by counting the words in both *The Brethren at Work* and its competitor *The Primitive Christian.* He found that a typical issue of the *The Primitive Christian* contained 25,165 words while the same issue for *The Brethren at Work* had only 20,393 words.

The editor of the *The Primitive Christian*, though happy to be ahead in the word count, was not greatly impressed. Henry B. Brumbaugh wrote: "We . . . hope that in the future there may be no call for such comparisons, as we think we are both publishing good church papers, fully worth the low price asked for them, and that true merit consists, not so much on the size of the sheet nor the number of the words, as upon the tone and character of the matter. . . . In the future, our leading object will be to labor harmoniously together for the good of the church and the promotion of the cause."

The Primitive Christian and Pilgrim,1877: 738-739.

80

Editors and Window-Looking

Visitors to the Brethren Publishing House, during the sixty years it was housed in downtown Elgin, Illinois, used to be fascinated by the printing, binding, and mailing activities, but many were not always clear as to what went on in the editorial offices. One good brother, when asked what he saw there, observed, "I don't see why they don't give Brother Moore [J. H. Moore, Gospel Messenger *editor] something to do. I passed his door repeatedly, but all he did was either write or read. All the others were working."*

During the time when Edward Frantz was editor, another visitor, a Pennsylvania farmer, was disappointed when he found Frantz gazing reflectively out the window. The visitor regarded that as a waste of time. Evidently he had not read many of Frantz's closely reasoned editorials.

In the early 1950s, Vernard Eller, the youthful editor of *Horizons*, had not yet earned his national reputation as a writer. Reflecting on the stories about Moore and Frantz, he noted that he could glean editorial ideas by looking out his window. A year later he almost gave up window-looking after he watched sign painters use the back wall of the Rialto Theater (located straight across the Fox River from the publishing house) for an advertisement showing an eighty-foot giant carrying nine-foot glasses of beer. The sign bore this message, "Meister Brau Beer—brewed for the likes of you."

Before he shut off the view, however, Eller's quick mind had translated Meister Brau into "The Master's Brew," and he was already comparing the glass of beer with Jesus' cup of suffering. Eller's editorial concluded, "The brew of the Master was bitter; there was nothing likeable in it. In fact he prayed that the cup would be taken from him. . . . So choose you this day which cup you will drink—the Meister Brau, brewed for the likes of you, or the Master's brew, brewed for the life of you."

The Brethren Encyclopedia. Philadelphia, Pa., and Oak Brook, Ill.: The Brethren Encyclopedia, Inc., 1983-84: 195 (sidebar).

Morse, Kenneth I. "Editors and Window-looking." *Messenger*, January 1983: 22.

Miller, J. E. *Stories from Brethren Life*. Elgin, Ill.: Brethren Publishing House, 1942.

Eller, Vernard. "Let's Face It . . . On Gazing the Window Out." *Horizons*, Jan. 28, 1951: 2.

Eller, Vernard. "Let's Face It . . . The Last Look Out the Window." *Horizons*, June 29, 1952: 2.

81

A Look into *The Inglenook*

The Inglenook *was published weekly from 1901 to 1913. It contained features of general interest, counsel for personal and family problems, editorial comment on church matters, and paid advertising.*

Turn-of-the-century advertising, which then was considered appropriate to a dignified, high-minded religious publication, strikes us now as almost flamboyant and, as far as patent medicines and land schemes are concerned, perhaps even fraudulent. Take the ad in *The Inglenook*, for example, for Victor Liver Syrup, "the great Family Medicine!" that laid claim to making some wonderful cures.

'Nook readers were offered, too, a free sample. "Send letter or postal for free sample HINDOO TOBACCO HABIT CURE. We cure you of chewing and smoking for 50¢, or money back." Advertisers were carefully reminded that *Inglenook* readers were nearly all well-to-do farmers.

Perhaps the most colorful and interesting ads in the periodical were those of land speculators who wrote in glowing terms of "100,000 ACRES OF GOVERNMENT

LAND! $1.25 per Acre. In the Delta of the Colorado, in San Diego County, California. Semi-tropical climate. The land is adapted to the growth of Alfalfa, Stock, Citrus and Deciduous Fruits."

Brethren were urged to settle in "the Brethren Colony, Quinter, Kansas" and to that purpose a full-page advertisement was placed on the inside cover of *The Inglenook*, complete with appropriate testimonials by Dunker residents.

> This colony is located in Gove County, Kansas, on the main line of UNION PACIFIC RAILROAD, 300 miles west of Kansas City. The town itself is composed principally of members of the Dunker church. It contains a post office, smithy, general stores, a two-story brick schoolhouse, and a neat and commodious Dunker church, seating about 500 people, free from debt, and including a membership of about 100. The surrounding country is largely settled up by members of the same church.

The good sisters of the Church of the Brethren and their friends were encouraged through *The Inglenook* to contribute their favorite recipes for its "Home Department." These recipes were gathered together to form the text of the *Inglenook Cook Book* published in 1901. The book, containing one thousand recipes, was an immediate success and continued to be used in Brethren and other kitchens for more than forty years. In 1970 the cookbook was reprinted from the original plates and is currently in print.

By 1940 the granddaughters of those who provided and used the original recipes were ready for their own cookbook, one that would again reflect their practical experience with recipes but that would also utilize up-to-date nutritional information. In 1941 they were invited to offer their best recipes for the new volume, and from the five thousand that were received, the recipes in this book were selected by committees of homemakers.

One of the interesting features of the turn-of-the-century publication, the *Inglenook Cook Book*, was its cover art, because it featured an attractive young lady who was properly adorned with a prayer covering and seemed acceptable to conservative readers. In the February 1985 issue of *Messenger,* editor Kermon Thomasson explains how he sought the identity of the cover girl from *Messenger* readers. Several responded, identifying the young woman as Anna Evans Wilson, the daughter of a Brethren family in Missouri. She eventually married a Baptist man and lived in Oakland, California.

Many modern-day Brethren would find it interesting to know that the editors of *The Inglenook* (1901–1913) were aware of the needs and concerns of youth then, as editors are today. Judging from this recipe for the good life, things have not changed all that much:

> Take your religion seriously; make it practical in everyday matters; don't force it on others; live at peace with your neighbors, those next door and those around the world; work hard; live simply; and always be prepared to lend more than one helping hand to someone in need.

Donovan, Jeanne. "The Inglenook: A Journal for a Gentler Time." *Messenger*, Sept. 10, 1970: 2-5. Expanded.

82

A Student Demonstration in the 1880s

The administrators of Mt. Morris College had to deal with a student demonstration long before the period of student unrest in the 1960s, In the early 1880s, this Brethren college in northern Illinois was contending with financial and leadership problems, still struggling to get on its feet. The burden of meeting obligations and dealing with deficits fell upon M. S. Newcomer, who had a major financial interest in the school. He decided the only solution was to sell the college property to the Studebaker brothers for a wagon factory. Solomon Z. Sharp, then the chairman of the faculty, tells what happened:

> This raised a storm from the students, citizens of Mt. Morris, and friends of the college. The students made a demonstration one night by drawing upon the campus the wagons and buggies of the town and placing large placards at each entrance to the campus with the inscription *Studebaker Wagon Factory.*
>
> The students of the literary societies, who had spent a considerable amount of money in furnishing their halls, also made a serious demonstration,

claiming that if the institution were sold, they would lose the money they had invested. The members of the faculty satisfied the students by guaranteeing to them the money they had invested in case the college should be sold. It was not sold.

The Brethren Encyclopedia. Philadelphia, Pa., and Oak Brook, Ill.: The Brethren Encyclopedia, Inc., 1983-84: 885 (sidebar).

Sharp, S. Z. *Educational History of the Church of the Brethren*, 1923.

83

Bethany Seminary: Four Locations—One Mission

In 1901 Albert C. Wieand and Emmanuel B. Hoff, who had become close friends at McPherson College, traveled together to the Holy Land. While on the Mount of Olives, overlooking the village of Bethany, they decided to start a Bible training school for the Brethren. "Kneeling under an olive tree, we named the unborn child Bethany Bible School . . . after the place where Jesus loved to come . . . and where people sat at his feet." Four years later, in 1905, the first classes were held in a frame house on Hastings Street in Chicago. Wieand and Hoff were among the first teachers. On October 30, 1994, after having roots in three Chicago-area locations, a new Bethany center was dedicated at Richmond, Indiana. Students and faculty share memories and visions of their seminary.

Hastings Street: A Glory That Will Not Go Away

Ernestine Hoff Emrick

At a mission church in a near-slum area close to the

Jewish ghetto of Chicago, twelve pupils and three teachers met to open Bethany Bible School. It was Tuesday, October 3, 1905. They had come to a school that had no money or endowment, or even any property. They were to live in neighborhood "flats" and hold classes in the home of one of the teachers, two of whom held none of the usual divinity degrees.

But they had something else. This seemingly inglorious beginning for a Bible school was deceptive. In fact, for those who could see it, there was a distinct aura of Glory about it—the kind of Glory that could make a school succeed in a day when the mortality rate for private schools was high indeed.

Nettie Senger

We were a group of country people who had never seen Chicago and were going into that city alone. We had to keep the front door locked but did not have eight keys. So we decided on a password. . . . I worked . . . in the Loop one day a week and got $1.25 a day. . . . I walked to work 2.5 miles to save carfare.

Hazel Moore Horner

We had a bathroom, cold as Greenland, with running water—ice water in winter. Classrooms were small, a bit on the dingy side.

Harry Brandt
Sacrifices were the order of the day. The teachers set the pattern.

J. Homer Bright
We got fish at the Jewish market . . . . Day-old bread was half-price, uncovered.

Anetta Mow
I have always felt it was good that Bethany was located in a great and "wicked" city in the very place where students could work firsthand with non-Christian forces.

Floyd Mallott
It was A. C. Wieand's dreams and loyalty to the Dunker church plus E. B. Hoff's saintliness of character and sound biblical scholarship . . . that guided Bethany in the early days. . . . What was a small beginning has blessed so many lives.

West VanBuren Street: From the Ridiculous to the Sublime

Chalmer Faw
My ties with Bethany span the years 1928–81 and run

the gamut from the ridiculous to the sublime—like the time beloved Professor Floyd Mallott started out for his weekend appointment in Grand Rapids with his briefcase in one hand and trash bag in the other. He arrived on the "L" platform with the trash only, his books having been thrown down into the incinerator!

A.C. Wieand was a great man of prayer. His testimony moved me deeply. The climax came in a chapel address shortly before he died in 1954. He was in his eighties, frail of body but vibrant in spirit. Raising his hand and lifting his husky voice, he said, "One of these days you are going to hear that Albert Wieand is dead. Don't you believe it. At that time I will be more alive than any of you!" Now if you go to the cemetery in Quinter, Kansas, and find the headstone marked FAW, you will see this epitaph inscribed in granite for both Mary and Chalmer: "More Alive Now Than Ever."

Garnett E. Phibbs

The first time this ole southern Virginia boy attended love feast in First Church, Chicago, I sat between a Chinese man and a Japanese man, and washed the feet of, hugged, and kissed a "Negro" man. What a mind-blowing culture shock! But I have never been more grateful for any experience of baptism-into-reality!

Curtis William Dubble

Dr. Warren Slabaugh in New Testament studies said, "What Jesus said, the way He acted, the way He related to God and persons, is more significant for my faith in Christ than the vehicle by which He came to earth." And Dr. William Beahm said, as we were discussing the glorious creation of humanity, "I don't know which is worse to say, that I came from a monkey or that I was made from mud."

E. Paul Weaver

I had reached Bethany with an anthropomorphic concept of God as a nice old man with a beard. I could sit on God's lap as I had my grandfather's and play with his beard. At first, when I heard clearly that D. W. Kurtz was talking about a God without a beard, I was about to call him an atheist. Since my father trusted Dr. Kurtz completely, I stayed with the class.

Dr. Kurtz had some habits that were different. When he hit the blackboard with the chalk to emphasize something, he sometimes broke the chalk. He was too rotund to pick up the broken chalk easily. He did not want to crush it on the floor. He usually did a neat little dance, kicking the pieces of chalk against the quarter round so that he would not make a mess on the floor.

The Boarding Club decided to invite the faculty to eat with us one night. After the meal we did skits on things that we saw in our different faculty members.

I was assigned to do Dr. Kurtz. “I’ve read a thousand books on the subject and I know! I know!” I lectured. Then I banged the chalk against the blackboard and did the dance, kicking the chalk against the wall. The next day in class, when Dr. Kurtz broke the chalk, he laboriously bent over and picked up the pieces. The whole class roared. I knew that I could get by with it without being down-graded because he knew how deeply I loved and respected him and his penetrating, well-organized mind.

Oak Brook: God Is Alive and Active in Suburbia

Kenneth L. Gibble

When William Hamilton came to the campus in 1965, he was one of the gurus of the “Death of God” movement. Several guys from the dorm (we were single and thus not weighed down with the cares of this world . . . in other words, we had some time for nonsense) decided to rig the large altar candle to go out during Hamilton’s lecture. The wick was cut just below the top of the candle. Sure enough, the candle sputtered and went out as Hamilton spoke. Dr. Paul Robinson, who knew nothing of skullduggery, noted the candle’s strange behavior. He commented on it at lunchtime, saying that he hoped this was not a "sign from on high." I'm not sure anyone admitted to the sabotage, but we had some good laughs about it.

James Merle Beckwith
I remember Dale Brown concluding a rousing lecture on the lively spread of Methodism across the continent with the westward flow of civilization, fairly shouting out, arms sweeping open to demonstrate, "and so the Gospel spread across the land like a wild fairy pire!" Then after a second of shock, realizing the switched consonants, he collapsed into his chair and quietly said, "Class dismissed."

Jean Lichty Hendricks
Bethany figures prominently in my memories and recollections. Some of my very first memories are of playmates in a Bethany apartment and on the Bethany grounds in Chicago.

One generation later, I was bearing my own children on Bethany's Oak Brook campus. My husband and I would literally meet each other on the sidewalk, infant daughter in one pair of arms, textbooks in another, and make a quick exchange: class for childcare! Our toddler-son first learned to crawl from one Bethany apartment to another, with an adult seeing that his mobility did not include a roll down the entry steps. We treasured the extended family that members of the Bethany community provided us as young parents.

Richmond, Indiana: A Day of New Beginnings

William Kidwell

Then I saw a new seminary and a new church, for the first Bethany and second Bethany had passed away, and soon this campus will be no more. And I saw the emerging school, new Bethany, coming down from Oak Brook to Richmond prepared as a gift fashioned for the church; and I heard a loud voice from the people saying, "Behold the power of God is with us, and we shall be God's people and the power of the Holy Spirit will sustain us; the comforter will wipe away every tear from our eyes, and our grieving shall cease, neither shall there be second guessing nor blaming nor despair anymore, for the former things have passed away." And God, hearing the voice of the people said, "Behold I make all things new." (paraphrase of Rev. 21:1-5)

Nancy Faus

After thirty years in Oak Brook, it's time for Bethany to move on, this time to a small city in Indiana in the midst of many Brethren congregations. May we not lose our commitment to urban ministry, cultural and racial diversity, and a worldwide church. Certainly, moving geographically will not diminish Bethany. The people, the learning, and the community spirit have made it the special place it is in the hearts of those who have walked its halls in Chicago, in Oak Brook, and who will walk its halls in Richmond. A deep love of Christ and a loyal commitment to the church go with us as we once again move on in faith.

The Brethren Encyclopedia. Philadelphia, Pa., and Oak Brook, Ill.: The Brethren Encyclopedia, Inc., 1983-84: 127 (sidebar).

Bethany: Memories & Visions (videotape). Bethany Theological Seminary, 1995.

84

A Precious Treasure Trove

Abraham Harley Cassel's unique collection of books, magazines, newspapers, tracts, and pamphlets was known to hundreds of historians, authors, professors, and editors, who came from great distances to consult him and examine his rare volumes. These people included Professor Edward B. Tyler of Oxford University, an archeologist, and Professor Oswald Seidensticker of the University of Pennsylvania. John Greenleaf Whittier, poet and journalist, was also a friend and correspondent, who turned to the Brethren antiquarian for source material for a poem called "The Pennsylvania Pilgrim."

Two Pennsylvania governors, both interested in history, often visited Cassel; they were M. G. Brumbaugh (1915-1919) and Samuel Pennypacker ((1902-1906). Brumbaugh was also a Brethren educator who dedicated his *History of the German Baptist Brethren* to Cassel, and Pennypacker wrote an acrostic sonnet on the name Abraham H. Cassel. The concluding portion of the sonnet not only honors Cassel but includes a reference to Christopher Sauer, Cassel's great-great-grandfather:

The "Hen-Medics"

C-heered by fond memories of men long dead,
A-t last, in garrets where the spiders wove
S-ecure he found the 'Christopher Saur' he sought,
S-o, while the twilight gathers 'round his head,
E-ach hour more precious grows his treasure trove,
L-ike joys by some hard self-denial bought.

The Brethren Encyclopedia. Philadelphia, Pa., and Oak Brook, Ill.: The Brethren Encyclopedia, Inc., 1983-84: 259 (sidebar).

Thomasson, Kermon. "Abraham Harley Cassel Cut a Wide Swath." *Messenger,* October 1978: 17-22.

Rosenberger, Elizabeth D. "Abraham H. Cassel," Parts 1,2,3. *Gospel Messenger,* 1908.

85

An Investment in Education

Many parents have sacrificed to educate their children, but few have been as thorough as Aaron I. Mow (1859–1925), a home missionary in Arkansas and Idaho. He packed up son Baxter and daughter Anetta in a covered wagon and drove them two hundred miles from their home in Weiser, Idaho, over the mountains to the University of Idaho. There the Brethren elder purchased an acre of land on which he started to build a small house before returning home. Baxter and Anetta finished the house, and it was their home for their four years at the university.

Soon after graduation in 1913, Baxter was awarded a Rhodes Scholarship for study at Oxford University. (The Weiser congregation had also called him to the ministry, but he was charged with irregular conduct because he insisted on wearing a necktie, and so he was deprived of his ministry.)

Once again Aaron Mow adjusted his personal plans to aid his children. He drove them to Chicago where Anetta could enter Bethany Bible School and Baxter could be off to Oxford, while the elder Mows went on to Florida.

Aaron Mow's effort to educate his children was rewarded by their lives of service. The Weiser congregation, becoming more tolerant of neckties, restored Baxter's ministry; and both Baxter and Anetta went as missionaries to India. *The Missionary Visitor*, in telling about Anetta's departure for the mission field in 1918, quite appropriately carried a picture of the building Aaron Mow provided for his children's university housing.

The Brethren Encyclopedia. Philadelphia, Pa., and Oak Brook, Ill.: The Brethren Encyclopedia, Inc., 1983-84: 891 (sidebar).

Sauger, W. H. and Agnes C. Kessler. "New Workers for Foreign Service." *The Missionary Visitor*, January 1918: 42-44.

Carter, Karen. "Baxter Mow: Twinkley-Eyed Scholar." *Messenger*, April 1977: 22-25.

86

Who Were the Four Horsemen?

Who were the "four horsemen" who visited Brethren camps in the 1920s? Certainly they bear no resemblance to the characters described in Revelation 6:1-8, though their visits were sponsored by the church and their venerable (and unreliable) Studebaker sedan was sometimes referred to as the "Sweet Chariot." For four summers, they traveled almost seven thousand miles at an average speed of thirty-five miles per hour.

Chauncey Shamberger had organized the youth program for the church and was responsible for developing Brethren camps. The second "horseman" was Dan West, who was preparing to take Chauncey's place as national youth director and was widely recognized as an outstanding discussion leader. The third was Alvin Brightbill, already exhibiting unique qualities as a music leader. The fourth "horseman" was Perry Rohrer, recreation leader, a psychologist who spent many years on the Bethany faculty and as a consultant for business firms. During the final weeks of their tour in 1929, they were joined by Joe Van Dyke, a teacher and inspirational writer for Brethren publications.

In her biography of Dan West, Passing on the Gift, *Glee Yoder explains how that particular summer of 1929 became legendary in Brethren camp history.*

Taking turns driving the "Sweet Chariot," . . . the Four Horsemen (plus Joe Van Dyke in 1929) usually traveled on Sundays to get to the next camp. An impromptu "Sunday service" evolved as they sang all the songs and hymns they could remember. Al strummed his guitar, though finding room for it was a problem with five men and their camp gear crammed together in the old car. In the midst of the songfest, Dan enjoyed telling about the black conscientious objector who stepped out of rank and sang a spiritual. His moving story usually called forth more seriousness in their singing as they bounced along day and night on the graveled roads . . . .

If something fell flat in a camp, they sought the reason for it and tried to avoid a recurrence. If one of them did something that did not appear to be quite right, it was brought out in the open. At one campfire where the visitors were noisy and failed to enter into the spirit of the camp, Chief [Chauncey] reprimanded them rather harshly. Later Dan very cautiously told Chauncey that he had overdone it a bit. . . .

Dan was joshed and teased about all the girl friends, always the prettiest ones, he found interesting in each camp. And was "Come, Ye Disconsolate" the only tune he could play on his violin? But there was a jovial and relaxed side to Dan. He seldom told a joke for humor's sake, but his deep, quiet understanding of humor was seen in the twinkle of his eyes. That he was always aware of humorous situations made him a good traveling companion. Perry, already interested in psychology, reflected on human behavior, sometimes irritating the group a bit. Joe? Joe was quiet but listened and thought a lot.

The most unpredictable driver turned out to be Dan, because he soon forgot what he was doing as his mind wandered to more important things. Plowing into a car near Columbus, Ohio, Dan, in his straightforward frankness, simply announced, "I hit 'im!"

Some summers prior to 1929, Dan had suggested that it might be helpful if, at the close of the camping season, each person would write the others an evaluation of their strengths and weaknesses. Though the comments were sometimes hard to take, they were given with love and received with acceptance. It was a rather ruthless experience, but through the years each expressed to the others a genuine appreciation for the insights given in these evaluations. . . .

The five had been close enough that frankness was accepted as their basis of understanding. Around the circle each one gave a critique of the others based on the summer's experience. When they came to Dan, one suggested that Dan's interest in people might not be as much in the person as in the functioning of his or her brain. Dan was a thinker, they counseled, and he respected people in proportion to their ability to keep up with him. All agreed with the observation.

It followed naturally that this same concern was related to Dan's relationship with the opposite sex. Four members of the team were married; Dan wasn't. They told him that at thirty-six he should be marrying. He had formed the habit, they said, of allowing some of the most beautiful and intellectual women all over the country to think he was in love with them. The group believed that he thought of them not as lovers, but minds. It was time for him to target in on some lovely person whose mind was good and who also had a heart. They assured Dan that the criticism of certain aspects of his personality was quite insignificant to the deep respect and love they all had for him. Because of the long and intimate friendship that existed among the team members, Dan was willing to take seriously what they urged. . . .

The young people were delighted with the camps and flocked to them in great numbers. Yet some members of the churches were not as happy with the camping program as were the young people. Al Brightbill once heard Dan being lashed with ugly words by a church leader "for helping our youth go to the dogs." But Dan in his characteristic way answered with soft words of empathy and with an understanding of the generation gap—even then when the older generation had the long hair and beards.

Dan had a strategy that worked at Camp Bethel in Virginia. One district in that area, which was not enthusiastic about camps for youth, sent a few of its board members to see what was going on. Dan suggested that the elders from the board and the campers play baseball during the recreation period. The visitors should do the batting; the young campers would run the bases for them. It was amazing how the visitors' attitudes changed when they participated with the youth and became part of the group. Discussions about camp and the youth program in that district seemed to change from then on.

Yoder, Glee. *Passing on the Gift: The Story of Dan West.* Elgin, Ill.: Brethren Press, 1978, 1995.

87

The "Hen-Medics"

Florence Gribble (1879–1942), a missionary physician in Africa for many years, told the story of her struggle to get a medical education in Chicago. Her male classmates objected strenuously to the presence of three women in their classes, the first women to be admitted to the Chicago Homeopathic College. So they took sections of human livers, hearts, lungs, and other vital organs and hurled them at the women students.

In another effort to force the young women to give up and leave, the male students formed an "Anti-Girl Society" to make life miserable for the "hen-medics." Whenever one of the women entered a classroom, she was greeted by applause, feetstomping, and sounds that resembled the cackling of hens. Florence Gribble later told how the young women responded:

> They decided that they would wait in the cloakroom until all were present, and then all enter the classroom at once. . . .This helped, at least, by the reduction of three serenades to one for each class, but the storm still continued. The girls decided to add smiles and bows to their defense. The young men could not long resist and gradually ceased to

oppose, thinking it more consistent with their dignity to assume an air of utter indifference to the presence of such an insignificant thing as a girl.

The Brethren Encyclopedia. Philadelphia, Pa., and Oak Brook, Ill.: The Brethren Encyclopedia, Inc., 1983-84: 810 (sidebar).

Gribble, Florence. *Stranger Than Fiction.* Winona Lake: Brethren Missionary Herald Co., 1949.

88

The Sinking of the *Zam Zam*

Three Brethren nurses en route to Nigeria were among the 120 missionaries on the Egyptian freighter *Zam Zam* when it was shelled by a German raider in the South Atlantic, April 17, 1941. They were Ruth Utz, Alice Engel, and Sylvia Oiness. The passengers were already apprehensive about traveling in a thirty-year-old ship under wartime blackout, but they would have been more alarmed had they known the boat was carrying contraband. The Germans knew it, and they shelled the ship without warning.

As the passengers prepared to enter lifeboats, some of them were pushed aside by frightened crew members. Although the *Zam Zam* was severely damaged and was later scuttled by the Germans, no one was killed during the attack or in the confusion of abandoning ship. The missionaries prayed and sang hymns; those who had managed to snatch their Bibles before leaving shared them with others. Their faith sustained them through a month on a German prison ship, the *Dresden*. Some of the *Zam Zam's* passengers were sent to prison camps in Europe, but the Americans (the U.S. had not yet entered the war) were taken to Portugal from German-occupied France, when the *Dresden* made land, and returned to New York on ships crowded with refugees.

The Brethren Encyclopedia. Philadelphia, Pa., and Oak Brook, Ill.: The Brethren Encyclopedia, Inc., 1983-84: 863 (sidebar).
The New York Times, June 22, 1941.
"The Sinking of the *Zam Zam.*" General Mission Board pamphlet.
Thomasson, Kermon. "The Night They Sank the *Zam Zam.*" *Messenger,* April 1981: 12-15.

89

God Works for Good

About a year after Nettie Senger arrived in China in 1916 as a young, single missionary, still busy with language studies, she decided that she must establish closer ties with the villagers, especially the women of Shansi Province. It was not enough to be recognized as "religious teacher Senger." Nettie soon arranged short trips away from the mission station to stay overnight in Chinese homes. She learned to accept strange customs without comment, including wearing the padded cotton gowns worn by the Chinese women. She carried her knitting with her so that she could share in their activities.

Some senior missionaries warned Nettie against identifying too much with local customs lest she "demean the dignity of a Christian missionary." But she ignored such well-meaning advice, just as she refused to be daunted by the dangers a single foreign woman faced in traveling where some male missionaries were reluctant to go.

Nettie Senger's adventures were not limited to riding a donkey over treacherous roads. Concerned for the plight of Chinese women, she established a school for young mothers and wrote textbooks that were used in many schools. Before war and revolution brought an abrupt end to Nettie's work in China in 1939, she had earned an M.A. degree in Chinese philosophy and a doctorate that focused on the impact of Chinese civilization on women.

One of Nettie's favorite Bible verses was Romans 8:28: "We know that all things work together for good for those who love God, who are called according to his purpose." Shortly before her death in Fort Wayne, Indiana, in 1969, she told her pastor that in spite of many frustrations, she loved all her work in China, because "God works for good."

Morse, Kenneth I. "Count Well the Cost." *Messenger*, June 1983: 20.

90

A Correction for Ripley

The widely syndicated newspaper column Ripley's "Believe It or Not!" devoted part of its October 30, 1975, feature to Mai Sule, a longtime leader in the Church of the Brethren in Nigeria. The feature was in error in identifying Mai Sule as the son of the ruler of the Pabir tribe who renounced his succession to power in order to become a Christian pastor.

Messenger set the record straight in 1976 by explaining that Mai Sule's father was at one time in line to become ruler but had fallen from favor. The title went to Mai Sule's great-uncle, then to his uncle, and finally to his first cousin. The *Messenger* report added, "Mai Sule's story, nevertheless, is a dramatic one, presented some years ago in the film *The African Prince*. He has been a leader in Lardin Gabas for many years, as well as its foremost hymn writer and music leader, and is familiar to many Brethren from his fraternal visit to the U.S. in 1972."

The Brethren Encyclopedia. Philadelphia, Pa., and Oak Brook, Ill.: The Brethren Encyclopedia, Inc., 1983-84: 782 (sidebar).
"Outlook." *Messenger*, February 1976: 6.

Sparks from the Hoff Anvil

—Brethren personalities

91

"The Touch of the Master's Hand"

Many collections of best-loved poems include "The Touch of the Master's Hand," written in 1921 by Myra Brooks Welch and first published that year in *The Gospel Messenger.* The author had heard a speaker explain how quite ordinary objects can be transformed in the hands of an expert. Her poem, recounting the story of an old violin considered worthless until it was played by a master musician, appealed to readers far beyond the Church of the Brethren. Soon it was copied and read and recited widely, frequently without credit to author or publisher. It was often included in anthologies and printed as a tract with the designation "Author Unknown."

In 1936 a speaker at an international YMCA conference read the poem and paid tribute to the "unknown" author, unaware that Dwight O. Welch, the poet's son, was presiding at the meeting.

Myra Brooks Welch was forced to give up plans for a career in instrumental music when she was confined to a wheelchair because of arthritis. Turning to poetry, she contributed verse to Brethren and other publications. Two collections of her poetry were published by

Brethren Press, one of them using as a title that of her most famous poem. After the book was published in 1941, the poem has more often been properly credited, and it continues to appear in magazines and books and is heard occasionally as the lyric of songs aired on the radio.

The Brethren Encyclopedia. Philadelphia, Pa., and Oak Brook, Ill.: The Brethren Encyclopedia, Inc., 1983-84: 1040 (sidebar).
Hollinger, Mrs. Albert. "The Story of a Poem." *Gospel Messenger,* Nov. 7, 1959: 8.
Garber, Mary and others. *Brethren Trail Blazers.* Elgin, Ill.: Brethren Press, 1960.

92

Sparks from the Hoff Anvil

Emanuel B. Hoff (1860–1928) had a facility for making short but pointed comments that students easily remembered. His son and biographer, Ernest G. Hoff, explained that his was a gift, but a carefully disciplined one, for the Bethany teacher often recorded in his notebooks the colorful expressions that occurred to him. Following are several of his best remembered sayings:

A good cry of penitence yields a good crop of trust.

Not many of us are good enough to have enemies.

Some sermons are mostly introduction with nothing to follow—big porch and little house.

Tithing is one-tenth of what we should do.

The only church organization that Jesus had was one hub and twelve spokes.

You can't understand unless you have a place to stand.

If the Christian is a farmer, every cow should bawl for the kingdom of God, every sheep should bleat for the kingdom, and every pig should squeal for it.

Some people are more sheep-wise or hog-wise than otherwise.

Boil down your writing until it makes good thick molasses, at least, if you can't make crystals.

If your theology doesn't fit the Bible, you had better change your theology.

The Brethren Encyclopedia. Philadelphia, Pa., and Oak Brook, Ill.: The Brethren Encyclopedia, Inc., 1983-84: 617 (sidebar).

Hoff, E. G. *Emanuel B. Hoff, Bible Teacher.* Elgin, Ill.: Brethren Publishing House, 1943.

93

Raspberry Seeds: the Quotable William Beahm

William Beahm (1896–1964) is affectionately remembered—by Brethren and others who knew him—for his quick wit and warm humor. Here are a few examples.

On prayer: It is not prayer that changes things. God does. It is something like a long belt on a threshing machine. The belt does not change things, the tractor does.

On trinity: The trinity is like a three-legged milking stool. The whole stool is God, and the legs are the Father, the Son, and the Holy Spirit.

On elders: An elder is an overseer and a supervisor according to the New Testament. What that means is that a good elder knows what to oversee and what to overlook.

On Solomon: Solomon was supposed to be so wise, but can you imagine day after day walking into the bathroom and getting tangled up in a thousand pairs of nylons?

On sin: Sin is central, not peripheral, in the experience of man. You can't clean up the water by painting the town pump.

On the church: When a church comes alive it has problems. A dead church is easy to serve. The easiest part of the church to manage is the cemetery.

On teaching a course on basic doctrines: I gave them "hell" yesterday. I've got to give them "heaven" today.

The Brethren Encyclopedia. Philadelphia, Pa., and Oak Brook, Ill.: The Brethren Encyclopedia, Inc., 1983-84: 101 (sidebar).

Fike, Earle W., Jr. *A Raspberry Seed Under God's Denture.* Elgin, Ill.: Brethren Press, 1979.

94

"More Than You Promise"

"Owe no man anything but to love one another." This biblical motto over John Clement Studebaker's blacksmith shop near Ashland, Ohio, reflected the Dunker principles of John, his wife Rebecca Mohler, whom he met at a Brethren meeting, and the church that met in their home in the late 1830s. These principles also made an impression on a growing family that included five sons who were later to launch the Studebaker Company, builder of wagons and automobiles.

Working with metal was part of the Studebaker heritage. The family included cutlery-makers in Solingen, Germany, long before two brothers, Peter and Clement, and their cousin Henry, arrived along with other Brethren from Germany at Philadelphia in 1736. John Clement (1799–1877), the father of the five best known Studebakers, lived first in Pennsylvania. Here he built a Conestoga wagon to carry his household to Ohio in 1836 and several years later to South Bend, Indiana, where the historic wagon can still be viewed in a museum.

By 1878 [the Studebakers] were considered to be the leading wagon makers of the world. By 1897 their company had manufactured three-fourths of a million vehicles, and this was several years before they produced their first gasoline and electric motorcars.

The rapid development of a successful business created some tensions between some of the Studebaker brothers and their church. Because they built wagons for the military, they were visited and admonished by Brethren deacons. Henry, the most Brethren of the five, could not approve of building wagons for the U.S. army to use in suppressing the Mormons who had earlier bought wagons from their company, so he sold his interest and retired to farming. The father, John Clement, discouraged his youngest son, Jacob, from serving in the Civil War.

With all of their enterprise, the Studebaker brothers remembered another of their father's mottoes, "Always give a little bit more than you promise." A biographer of John Mohler Studebaker, the brother who continued with the business until shortly before his death in 1917, said of him that "the old Dunkard frugality never entirely disappeared." Over the mantle at his office in South Bend was a painting of his boyhood home and on his desk was a picture of his father.

The Brethren Encyclopedia. Philadelphia, Pa., and Oak Brook, Ill.: The Brethren Encyclopedia, Inc., 1983-84: 1230 (sidebar).

Carlock, W. A., and others. *The Studebaker Family in America, 1736-1976.* Tipp City, Ohio: Studebaker Family National Association, 1976.

95

Falling Among Thieves

Albert Cassel Wieand (1871–1954), founder and president of Bethany Bible School, must have often recounted Jesus' story of the man who "fell among thieves" while traveling from Jerusalem to Jericho (Luke 10:30-37). But for A.C. Wieand and Katherine Broadwater Wieand, whose travels took them beyond Jericho, to fall among thieves was not just an episode in a story. It happened to them.

During a visit to the Holy Land in the fall of 1910, the Wieands joined seven other tourists on a trip they hoped would encircle the entire Dead Sea area. However, at Kerak, the capital of ancient Moab, they were caught in an insurrection of Arabs against the Turks. Thinking they were protected by friendly guards, the tourists sought to return to Jerusalem, but on the way they were kidnaped by a hostile band of Arabs.

Their money and equipment were taken at gunpoint, and they were threatened with death. The bandits tried to divert the group from the main road into a swamp, but the travelers after a time were able to continue on the right path. Finally, after many harrowing adventures, they were rescued by friendly Arabs.

In his biography of A. C. Wieand, V. F. Schwalm recounts the dangers that faced the Wieands: “It seems the good Lord certainly had his arms around our friends. When they approached Jerusalem they could say . . . ‘As the mountains are round about Jerusalem, so the Lord is round about his people, henceforth and evermore.’ ”

The Brethren Encyclopedia. Philadelphia, Pa., and Oak Brook, Ill.: The Brethren Encyclopedia, Inc., 1983-84: 1344 (sidebar).

Schwalm, V. F. *Albert Cassel Wieand.* Elgin, Ill.: Brethren Press, 1960.

96

Man of Many Gifts

In 1877, soon after becoming Juniata College's first teacher of art, David Emmert made the acquaintance of J. C. Blair, a storekeeper in Huntingdon, Pennsylvania, who wanted to sell wallpaper products. During the course of their conversation that day, Emmert occupied himself by fashioning a pad that he intended for taking notes while auditing another professor's class. He used a piece of stiff cardboard for backing and then added a stack of papers, which he clamped together with four large carpet tacks.

It was this homemade pad that inspired the "Blair Tablet" and a whole new stationery industry. A year or so later, the tablet caught on, especially in public schools. Then Emmert designed the "Keystone trademark," a design still carried on some paper products. Blair offered Emmert a half interest in his growing business, but Emmert declined, for he was far more interested in providing good homes for orphans.

As a boy and as an apprentice at a manufacturing company, Emmert was concerned about the horrors experienced by children in Baltimore and their plight when abandoned and left to the mercy of local institutions. Juniata College historian Earl Kaylor says, "He told how children were made to mingle with all kinds of people—degenerate, deranged—and often denied a wholesome family life." This situation repulsed him.

So Emmert, as a humanitarian, developed a sound plan for the care of children. He was insistent that orphan children had a right to be well treated. The unique features of his child welfare plan, widely accepted as the Huntingdon Idea, were that children receive not only personal attention, but the financial support of a community that would provide an endowment for them. Much of Emmert's time was given to developing orphanages in Huntingdon, Pennsylvania, and Hagerstown, Maryland.

In a privately printed booklet, "The Huntingdon Idea, a Sound Plan for Children," Professor Kaylor emphasizes that David Emmert could have gained financially from his inventions as a designer and teacher and his popularity as a writer.

Emmert's talents as a writer and artist are evident in his attractive account of Juniata's first twenty-five years, a record rich in stories of human interest and amply illustrated by the artist-author. But for David, finding homes for orphans became the passion that determined the total investment of his life.

David Emmert, who worked hard and endangered his health, died in 1911 at age fifty-six. His close friend, W. J. Swigart, wrote an eloquent tribute to Emmert, describing him as a man who literally lived for others in the ways depicted in Matthew 25.

> Professor Emmert did not merely write and speak and send people as agents for his child welfare work. He went himself. To the hungry, he carried food; the naked he clothed; those in prison and sick he visited and ministered to. No home was too lowly, no poverty and squalor were too abject; no vice and sin were so gross as to bar his entrance if he believed he could help. No hour was too late; no road too rough or muddy; no night too dark for his feet to go on errands of mercy; his own hands washed and cleansed the diseased and filthy; and his own arms carried the little ones to places of comfort.

The Brethren Encyclopedia. Philadelphia, Pa., and Oak Brook, Ill.: The Brethren Encyclopedia, Inc., 1983-84: 235 (sidebar).
Kaylor, Earl C., Jr. "The Versatile David Emmert." A privately printed brochure.
Kaylor, Earl C., Jr. *Truth Sets Free*. South Brunswick: A. S. Barnes, 1977.

97

Pole-Vaulting Preacher

Sportswriters called him “Pole-Vaulting Parson,” “Vaulting Vicar,” and “Decathlon Deacon.” In the late 1940s and early 1950s, Robert “Bob” Richards, a Church of the Brethren minister, competed in three Olympics (winning a gold medal in 1956) as a pole vaulter.

After his sixty-fifth competitive attempt, Richards cleared fifteen feet, the second pole vaulter in history to do so, and he continued to equal that record over a hundred times. In 1951 Richards won the Sullivan Award as the amateur athlete of the year; that same year he was also the U. S. national decathlon champion. At the time he was an instructor at La Verne College in California.

Richards grew up in Champaign, Illinois, where he was a member of a local gang, five of whom later went to prison. Instead of following their course, Richards became active in the Champaign Church of the Brethren. With the encouragement of its pastor, Merlin Garber, he went on to Bridgewater College and Bethany Theological Seminary and later became pastor of the Long Beach, California, congregation.

Preaching in a Tavern

Always in demand as an inspirational speaker (he used to average five hundred speeches a year), he held many evangelistic meetings and spoke at many Brethren gatherings, including Annual Conference, as well as at schools, service clubs, and athletic events. He also made television commercials for a well-known breakfast cereal. At the height of his sports activity, Richards would tell reporters, "I can sincerely say I owe my athletic achievements to the power of the Lord," and he often mentioned that he was converted at age sixteen. He once said, "I never amounted to much as an athlete, a student, or an individual until I was converted to religion. Christianity builds a total personality."

In June 1984, Richards announced his candidacy for president of the United States under the auspices of the newly formed Populist Party. Known as a motivational speaker, he observed, "I can speak right to the issues, and I don't have to worry if I'm going to win."

The Brethren Encyclopedia. Philadelphia, Pa., and Oak Brook, Ill.: The Brethren Encyclopedia, Inc., 1983-84: 70 (sidebar).

Richards, Bob. *The Heart of a Champion.* Ada, Mich.: Fleming H. Revell, 1959.

98

A Fortissimo Man

When Albert T. Ronk (1886–1972) was just a small boy, he demonstrated an amazing understanding of machinery and mechanical processes that would be evident throughout his long career as pastor, evangelist, historian—and inventor. At age four he described to his amazed parents how a steam locomotive runs. At age five he made himself so obnoxious by always explaining machinery that his family told him, "You've got wheels in your head."

Those busy wheels in Albert Ronk's brain were set in motion, he said, because he always asked, Why? As a youth he developed ingenious devices for sawing wood and running a steam engine. He made his own mechanically powered well-drilling rig and devised a number of other machines to aid California farmers. A call to the ministry drew him to Ashland College in Ohio, where he perfected a mechanical atomizer used for medicinal applications. While serving in a pastorate in Indiana, he brought electricity to homes and businesses in a small town that previously had no lights. The scope of his inventing was almost as wide as the necessities that prompted such devices as a manure loader, a steel folding chair, a power shovel, a refuse burner, and a switch control for a poultry brooder.

Though Ronk was busily engaged for many years in inventing new machines and developing the factories, plants, and mills that used them, he continued his evangelistic and pastoral work as opportunities came. For relaxation he turned to what he enjoyed most. "Down in my shop, alone, I can whittle, and file, and drill, and turn, and what have you. The rhythm of motion and the whir of motor is music to thought—a sort of symphony of cogitation."

While Albert Ronk was still a relatively young man, an article in *The Brethren Evangelist* (1917) described him as a "mechanical genius and preacher . . . a fortissimo man dealing in ultimates." Fifty years later those ultimates were clearly articulated in his writings on the beliefs and practices, the program and the history of the Brethren Church, entitled *Search for Truth*.

The Brethren Encyclopedia. Philadelphia, Pa., and Oak Brook, Ill.: The Brethren Encyclopedia, Inc., 1983-84: 660 (sidebar).

Ronk, A. T. *Search for Truth*. Ashland, Ohio: Brethren Publishing Co., 1973.

99

Blindness No Handicap

When Peter Keyser, Jr. (1766–1849) was a young man, he was put to work grinding bark for his father's tannery. Eager to learn the scriptures, the younger Keyser placed a shelf above his work on which he put an open Bible and began memorizing long sections of the Bible. Over a period of years, he completely memorized the New Testament and major portions of the Old Testament, including all the Psalms, the prophetic writings, and the Pentateuch.

Later in life, as a lumber merchant, Keyser would rise at four in the morning and study before the day's business began. Such diligent study may have contributed to his being blind in his advanced years. But blindness was no handicap for the preacher who could announce a chapter and repeat it from memory without missing a word. People who knew him often said that if the scriptures were destroyed by accident, Peter Keyser could replace them from memory.

The Brethren Encyclopedia. Philadelphia, Pa., and Oak Brook, Ill.: The Brethren Encyclopedia, Inc., 1983-84: 692 (sidebar).

Howe, Roland. *The History of a Church.* Philadelphia: n.p., 1943.

100

An Episode in Modern Medical History

As a young registered nurse, Laura Wine was rejected for overseas mission service because she once had tuberculosis. Finally, after retiring from a career in nursing in the Chicago area, she was then accepted for volunteer service in Nigeria at a Church of the Brethren mission hospital. When she died in 1969 after a brief but severe illness, missionaries and doctors suspected a previously undiscovered viral disease that was later named Lassa Fever after the hospital where Laura Wine, its first victim, served as a volunteer.

Author John G. Fuller, describes the search for the causes of Lassa Fever. In preparation for writing *Fever*, his best-selling account of a four-year struggle to identify the deadly virus, Fuller covered the Church of the Brethren mission area, interviewed doctors and workers, and visited Brethren and Sudan Interior Mission hospitals. He also contacted university laboratories and public health offices in many countries. Fuller's account begins with Laura Wine's illness, of which he writes, "Neither she nor anyone else knew at the time that her malaise and backache would set into motion one of the most frightening episodes of modern medical history. It would reach from Africa to the United States in a series of unpredictable incidents that was to bring into action many of the leading medical scientists in the world."

Fuller did not hesitate to size up the missionaries he met while researching his book. "They believe what they preach and they believe it literally. Their inner faith may sometimes seem manic or overly euphoric, but its sincerity cannot be doubted. The extent of their works is reflected in the impressive hospitals, schools, dispensaries, and churches they have carved out of the deep bush."

John Hamer was the only doctor at Lassa during Laura Wine's final months there. He and his wife, Esther, observed that "Laura's giving of her life, which she was totally prepared to do for the sake of Christian service and medical advancement, was a symbol of love. Love made the difference all the way for her."

"News." *Messenger,* April 23, 1970: 16-17.
"Outlook." *Messenger,* May 1974: 4-5.
"Outlook." *Messenger,* June 1974: 8-9.
Hamer, John and Esther. "Lassa Fever: The Story of a Killer Virus" (a book review). *Messenger,* July 1974: 24-27.

101

Inventive Genius

Samuel Fahrney (early 1800s) lived a quiet life as a deacon among the Brethren in Washington County, Maryland. Never as well known as his father, the "walking doctor" who ministered to the sick in the early years of the nineteenth century, or his nephew who made a fortune selling patent medicines, Samuel turned his ingenuity toward inventing such practical devices as a garlic press, a washing machine, a sausage grinder, and a molasses faucet. Of greater significance to the American economy was his pioneering work in developing a reaper that could be transported easily. According to tradition, he took his machine to Rockbridge County, Virginia, where it was demonstrated in a field of oats. There he exchanged ideas with young Cyrus Hall McCormick, a Virginian who patented an improved model of his reaper in 1834 and who later moved to Chicago, where he set up a factory for the manufacture of reapers. Though Fahrney failed to get a patent for his reaper, he contributed to the beginnings of the mechanical revolution in agriculture.

The Brethren Encyclopedia. Philadelphia, Pa., and Oak Brook, Ill.: The Brethren Encyclopedia, Inc., 1983-84: 466 (sidebar).

Henry, J. Maurice. *History of the Church of the Brethren in Maryland,* 1936.

102

The Peace Connection

In the late 1940s, John H. Eberly, a former Brethren pastor and public school teacher, strongly believed a foreign exchange program for high school youth would encourage peacemaking. So with the approval of the Brethren Service Commission, he organized the first program for German youth to spend a year in Brethren homes in America. During the next few years, more than one thousand German youth participated, and in the years to follow, a similar number of Brethren youth from this country spent a year in European homes and schools, thus making it a genuine exchange program.

In 1956 the program was enlarged to include young people from other denominations and sponsoring agencies and was named the International Christian Youth Exchange (ICYE).

When the exchange students returned to their homelands overseas, they found their lives changed in many ways. In 1964, without informing John Eberly of their intentions, they formed an organization called the John Eberly-Gesellschaft (John Eberly Society). They established an international office and regularly published a journal called *The Echo,* which carries mostly German contributions on many issues as well as the names and addresses of exchanges both in the United States and overseas. Former exchange students, many of them now in leadership positions in their own countries, attest to their respect for John Eberly as a man and as a leader who helped their lives. One of the German students describes the feeling they had for John:

> A man is a man is a man is a man,
> you came and you acted and you convinced and you pioneered,
> you cared and you loved and you accepted and you reconciled,
> you shared and you saved and you assisted and you delivered,
> now we know a man from a man.

While John Eberly probably understood this kind of personal tribute, he was undoubtedly more pleased with the way in which the students reflected the purposes of his life through their efforts for mutual understanding and peace among nations. John Eberly's greatest satisfaction came not from having his name attached to an organization as much as from the realization that the values he sought in developing the exchange program were accepted by the young people who participated. The following statement appeared both in German and English in *The Echo:*

> Your head belongs into the last category. And your character definitely corresponds to your head. Initiating and organizing the students' exchange program was truly the deed of a pioneer. Even though you did not conquer new land as the first pioneers in your country did, you definitely conquered new hearts in the only battle that you as a pastor of the church of the Brethren could fight: in the battle for mutual understanding and peace among nations. The only battle, but at the same time the most worth-while battle that can be fought in our world.

Eberly, William R. "Eberly, John H." *The Brethren Encyclopedia.* Philadelphia, Pa., and Oak Brook, Ill.: The Brethren Encyclopedia, Inc., 1983-84.

The Echo, October 1964, No. 3.

103

He Ate the Whole Thing

Many people who knew Brother I. N. H. Beahm (1859–1950) have stories to tell about him. One storyteller, Dottie Murray, says, "I rather suspect that some of the tales about him got dressed up a wee bit, but I am convinced in my own mind that he was one of the greats of our early heritage, eccentricities and all." Murray goes on to share these stories of I. N. H. Beahm:

Big-meeting time (the fall Communion) was one of the more important events of the year in our household. There were often guests—many of them—staying overnight following Communion and for Sunday dinner. Early Saturday morning was a busy time for an older sister who baked cakes and pies for the occasion. Upon returning home from Communion Saturday evening about 9:00, Mother asked the two ministers staying overnight with us (Brother Beahm was one of them) if they would care for a bite to eat before retiring. They assured her they weren't really hungry but would appreciate a glass of milk and perhaps a bite of something sweet. Twelve-year-old Louise, justifiably proud of her beautiful, four-layer, fresh coconut cake, brought the cake in so they could serve themselves a small bite, whereupon Brother Beahm and the other minister devoured the entire cake while carrying on a two-hour theological discussion with our father. No doubt they may have had a little help from him, but since our father was not a big cake-eater, Louise always declared that it was Brother Beahm who made her culinary pride disappear crumb by crumb. (Maybe the grief was all the greater because she knew that she would have to be up before five on Sunday morning to bake another cake before Sunday dinner.)

Another story has it that because of his short stature and a slight hearing problem, Brother Beahm always sat on the front pew at most services. Arriving at one of our district conferences after the service had started, he did not want to march to the front during the worship service, so he waited quietly in the rear of the church until the offering was lifted. During the interlude of prayer for the offering, Brother Beahm quietly crawled on his hands and knees to the front of the church, and when the "Amen" was said, there he was, seated on the front pew as usual, probably looking like a saucy little elf that had just put one over on the people who wondered how he got there.

104

The Making of a Brumbaugh

The man who became governor of Pennsylvania in 1915 and was promoted as a "favorite son" candidate for the presidency in 1916 revealed early in life many of the qualities that marked him as a leader. Yet, according to Brumbaugh's most recent biographer, Earl Kaylor, Jr., that leadership was tested most severely in the need to reconcile political realities with the principles of a peace church.

When Martin Grove Brumbaugh was eight years old, he upset the careful plans of the James Creek Sunday school to encourage Bible memorization. The Pennsylvania congregation offered a red card for each remembered verse and a blue card for ten correctly recited. Martin took most of one class period to recite 145 verses from memory, capturing a year's supply of cards and demonstrating his eagerness for learning.

When Martin was eighteen, he helped his father secure twelve hundred logs for telegraph poles for the Pennsylvania Railroad. After they were assembled on a river, ready to be delivered, a violent storm came that scattered them for great distances. For weeks father and son searched for their lost logs and finally replaced all that were missing. The next year, when Martin was running for county superintendent of schools—the first of many responsible jobs he held as an educator—a farmer who was committed to supporting Brumbaugh's opponent asked him, "Are you any relation to that young Brumbaugh who helped his father with the telegraph poles?" Martin's affirmative answer won the farmer's vote—and the election—by just one vote.

The Brethren Encyclopedia. Philadelphia, Pa., and Oak Brook, Ill.: The Brethren Encyclopedia, Inc., 1983-84: 223 (sidebar).

Flory, Claude R. "M. G. Wants Me for a Sunbeam." *Brethren Life and Thought*, Vol. XXI (1976):121-128.

Kaylor, Earl C., Jr. *Martin Grove Brumbaugh.* Cranbury, N.J.; Associated University Presses, 1996.

Trumbull, Charles Gallaudet. "The Making of a Brumbaugh." *The Sunday School Times*, Dec. 16, 1905.

105

A Man of Property and Principle

The young German immigrant lost no time in establishing himself in the colonies. Arriving at Philadelphia in 1750, Jacob Bromback (Brumbach) settled soon afterward near Hagerstown, Maryland. Some Brethren historians have speculated that he was present in April 1755, when General Edward Braddock met with Benjamin Franklin (who hoped to obtain needed supplies from Pennsylvania colonists) and young George Washington (who was to serve as an aide to the general) to plan Braddock's ill-fated campaign to capture Fort Duquesne.

One report suggests that Braddock's army camped near Bromback's farm while the general and perhaps also his aide stayed with the young German. Another report claims that Braddock offered Bromback a commission, which he refused on religious principles, yet he agreed to join the expedition as a packman and also to help with the sick and the wounded. If the report is true, he may have cared for Braddock, who was killed, and he may have nursed George Washington, who became seriously ill.

Whatever Bromback's principles may have been in 1755, the records show that in 1760 he married a

Brethren woman and later united with her church. He must have held to his nonresistant standards during the Revolutionary War since he and his son were fined in 1776 "for not enrolling in the Cause."

Both before and after the war, Bromback was unusually adept in acquiring land; it is said that he owned more than six thousand acres in Bedford and Blair Counties in Pennsylvania, as well as large tracts in Frederick County, Maryland.

While it is doubtful that his example persuaded Washington to work for religious liberty—as some Brethren have surmised—Bromback certainly provided the land base for a multitude of descendants who built churches and became leaders in the church he chose.

The Brethren Encyclopedia. Philadelphia, Pa., and Oak Brook, Ill.: The Brethren Encyclopedia, Inc., 1983-84: 516 (sidebar).

Ankrum, Freeman. *Sidelights on Brethren History.* Elgin, Ill.: Brethren Press, 1962.

Henry, J. M. "Pathfinders in Maryland." *Gospel Messenger,* April 28, 1934: 7-8.

Henry, J. M. *History of the Church of the Brethren in Maryland,* 1936.

106

Life at Full Throttle

Otho Winger, president of Manchester College from 1911 to 1941, is described by one college historian as a man who drove with the throttle wide open, full of vibrant energy. Winger's successor and biographer, Dr. Vernon Schwalm, tells us more about the man.

It was common knowledge that Otho Winger was an indefatigable worker. One had to be endowed with an iron constitution and blessed with boundless physical energy to stand up under the strain as long as he did. . . .

[Winger] often went to the office before breakfast and worked awhile, returned after breakfast, worked all morning, all afternoon, and at night until twelve, one, or two o'clock. This schedule was followed for many, many years. . . .

Winger was cast in a heroic mold—in every sense. Physically he was strong, rugged, massive, masculine. . . . His voice carried well—too well at times. It could be heard through the halls and corridors, "booming," as some said. On one occasion, after succeeding Winger as president of the college, V. F. Schwalm heard loud talking in the hall during chapel. When he went to quiet the noise, he found President Winger talking to one of the professors. There was no rebuke! . . .

President Winger was an individualist in every way. With his little lowly acts of unexpected kindness to students and faculty, his long hours in the office, his irregular habits of sleep, his fast driving—with an occasional automobile accident killing a cow or a horse and often nearly killing himself—his peculiar interest in old people, his Indian hobby, his thundering denunciation of sin and some sinners, and his tender ministrations to the sick or the bereaved, there developed a folklore about the president of Manchester—most of it very kindly if not really affectionate—which was an asset both to him and to the college. . . .

He disliked card playing and believed cards were the gambler's tool. Early in his presidency he confiscated cards when he found them. In his later years, he recognized that it was difficult to eliminate card playing entirely from the private rooms of students, but it was forbidden in the social functions of the school. . . .

He was opposed to the use of tobacco among college boys and girls. To a number of parents he wrote that he thought what got their boys into trouble was the use of tobacco. And in a case where a number of boys got into some other difficulty that led to disciplinary action, one of the conditions upon which they might continue in college was to cease smoking.

One of the strange contradictions in the life of President Winger was his severity in certain kinds of situations and his amazing patience and forgiveness in others. Where there was gross sin, the violation of a sacred trust, persistent theft, or cases of persistent flaunting of the rules of morality and common decency, President Winger was exceedingly severe. . . .

In other cases his patience and forbearance were so great that they led to the annoyance of the faculty. Many a boy was forgiven again and again. The president would secure a promise of improvement from him. If he erred again, he gave him another chance and yet others.

Schwalm, V. F. *Otho Winger, 1877-1946.* Elgin, Ill.: Brethren Publishing House, 1952. Adapted.

When Robert Ebey was a student at Manchester College, he served as President Winger's chauffeur during 1940–41. He tells the following story that illustrates President Winger's unique personality.

President Winger would walk over to our dorm office-apartment and would start talking even before he reached our door. "Ebey, can you be ready in a half hour to go to Ohio?" It could have been Michigan or Illinois. I would agree that I could.

Every time we started out we would go through the same conversation:

"What part of the state do we go to this time?"

"You drive the car. I'll tell you where to go."

"How long will we be gone?"

"I don't know. It depends on how much I get done and how tired I get."

Also, without fail, as soon as we would get to a main highway, I would ask, "How far do we follow this road?"

"You drive the car. I'll tell you where to go."

There was still another aspect of the trip that always took place. As we would start out, President Winger would say, "We will take it easy this trip. Keep the speed down to 55." If I would let the speed creep up to 60, President Winger would notice it and tell me to keep it on 55.

Without exception, the return trip was another story. "Ebey, the car seems to be running pretty good. Let's try 65."

Perhaps a half hour later, "Ebey, there isn't much traffic. Can you make it go 70 or 75?"

Preaching in a Tavern

One afternoon we were traveling 55 on a good gravel road in Ohio. All of a sudden, President Winger said, "Stop!" I could see nothing out of the way, so I started slowing down.

"*Now*, Ebey, when I say stop I mean STOP. I recognized a house back there and we have to make a call. Now we will have to turn around and go back. Ebey, when I say stop I mean STOP."

President Winger was one of the church's giant leaders. He continually kept us entertained and interested with his stories of the Indians of Indiana, of the church and of the college. I shall always cherish the times I drove for him to a preaching service, to a church dedication, on college field work. When that DeSoto had ten thousand miles on it, I figured I had driven all but about five hundred of the miles.

For all my work at the college, my official boss was L. D. Ikenberry, the college treasurer. One time I said to him, "I am supposed to be working full time here at the college. President Winger keeps asking me to drive for him."

L. D. Ikenberry replied, "Would you rather not drive for him?"

"Oh, no." I said, "I like to drive for him. I enjoy doing it. But when I am doing that, I am not getting my other work done here."

L. D. Ikenberry said with a smile, "President Winger needs a good driver. I think you should do it."

Ebey, Robert. *Preacher Bob*. Privately printed, 1990.

107

One of a Kind

By his own confession, Reuel Pritchett (1884–1974) was a unique person. He said, "God makes each of us individual if we don't stifle it, and I've tried not to." Many of his observations about himself, his environment, and his ministry are worth noting:

On enjoying life: A man who's a Christian isn't dragging his face: he enjoys all the cinnamon, pepper, and syrup of life.

On enjoying earth: The earth is a massive playhouse of Jehovah's mountains and plains, oceans and deserts, full of his birds and animals, insects and fish. All of this is God's creation and we are his custodians.

On preaching: Be sure you stand on both feet. Don't swamp. Cover the ground. . . . Your message should be fundamental, historical, philosophical, and biblical. Begin. Be brief. Be seated.

On collecting: I've spent four-fifths of a century drawing together ideas and facts that would otherwise have been lost. There's so much to investigate and preserve and examine and explain.

On dying: If I'm gonna have a Companion—and the Book says he will be with me to the end—I want to talk with him and have his comradeship through the oracles of death.

On living: This I do know, that I owe God more than I can imagine for being able to perceive, comprehend, enjoy—live. How wonderful it is to grace God's earth.

On time: Now is the day of salvation. The day of this world is far spent: it's after milking time on the clock of history.

The Brethren Encyclopedia. Philadelphia, Pa., and Oak Brook, Ill.: The Brethren Encyclopedia, Inc., 1983-84: 1061 (sidebar).
Pritchett, Reuel, with Dale Aukerman. *On the Ground Floor of Heaven.* Elgin, Ill.: Brethren Press, 1980.

108

In Search of Falling Stars

Many years before Americans lined up to glimpse a fragment of rock brought back from the moon, a young professor in a Brethren college had discovered a source of information from outer space. Harvey H. Nininger was on his way home from the McPherson College chapel in 1923 when a meteorite fell some distance away in brilliant light. Already curious about these "falling stars," he began a search for meteorites, leading eventually to what was reported to be the largest private meteorite collection in the world. He was once credited with finding half the meteorites then discovered in the world. After thirty-seven years of collecting, Nininger sold his meteorites to the British Museum in London and to Arizona State University at Tempe. At the latter institution, they were made available for research and study.

Nininger grew up in Kansas and Oklahoma, where his devout Brethren parents were slow to encourage his scientific inclination. Although he was nineteen years old before he was able to complete elementary school, he continued his education with great effort and with profit in knowledge and religious insight. In

1966 he told an interviewer, "The study and quest of meteorites have made me a more deeply religious man than before. I see God all around me."

The Brethren Encyclopedia. Philadelphia, Pa., and Oak Brook, Ill.: The Brethren Encyclopedia, Inc., 1983-84: 781 (sidebar).
Heatwole, Thelma. "Scientist in Quest of Stars." *Messenger,* Nov. 24, 1966: 6-8.

109

In the Front Seat with M. R. and Amy

From July 11 to August 7, 1958, I saw M. R. Zigler almost every day. The following observations relate to that experience.

In 1958 several people were designated by Annual Conference to represent the church at the 250th anniversary at Schwarzenau. The group included the 1958 moderator, Desmond Bittinger; the chairperson of the anniversary committee, Paul H. Bowman; representatives of Men's Work and Women's Work; representatives of overseas churches; and me as editor of the *Gospel Messenger*.

M. R. Zigler was eager for our delegation to appreciate the magnitude and the variety of the Brethren service program in Europe. He and Wilbur Mullen made plans for us to tour centers of Brethren activity in Europe; to visit government officials, interchurch agencies, reconstruction projects, work camps, and refugee centers; and to talk with church leaders, BVS volunteers, and the recipients of heifers and other aid. We were indeed favorably impressed, even overwhelmed, for it was evident that the Europeans with whom

Brethren had worked were profoundly grateful for aid and especially appreciative of our policy not to start new Brethren churches but to work with existing churches in Europe.

One of our meetings was held in the Zigler apartment at 16 Chateau Banquet, in Geneva, Switzerland. It was a spacious residence, regarded by some Brethren as far too lavish for a simple lifestyle. We met there with leaders of the Eastern Orthodox Church, the Lutheran World Federation, the Reformed and Presbyterian Alliance, the Baptist World organization, along with other World Council of Churches personnel. Despite the presence of so much "brass" from the various church hierarchies, M. R., in his usual manner, kept the sessions informal and down-to-earth. I learned later that such a meeting was rather unique in Geneva because the wives had been invited. Amy Zigler, in her warm and friendly way, treated everyone as if they were guests at a Brethren farmhouse dinner.

Several years later, a Lutheran journalist who worked with Lutheran World Federation in Geneva during the Zigler years told me that M. R. was truly unique among all the World Council and world church leaders. M. R. had none of the trappings of a professional churchman; was unimpressed by, if not actually ignorant of, ecclesiastical protocol; was a man who said precisely what he was thinking; and was a man whose convictions were persuasive because they were so much a part of him. This young journalist was especially impressed with M. R.'s forthrightness, especially when he continued to remind world church leaders that wars would cease if Christians from all nations would refuse to fight each other.

A young man named David Ellis traveled with us through Europe part of the time. David enjoyed driving fast over mountain roads, shocking older members of our party whenever he could. On several occasions M. R. challenged David to give his life to the church. Though quite serious in his challenge, M. R. was friendly and joking with David, enjoying his brash opinions. Their conversations continued for several days as M. R. persisted in seeking a commitment from David.

David Ellis did not enter Brethren Volunteer Service or become involved with any service-orientated movement then but went on to become a university president. Impressed with M. R. and his appeal, David expressed appreciation for the loving concern that M. R. showed for him as a person.

M. R. was constantly inviting young people like David to venture out into new areas of witness and service, but he often was not as patient with Brethren church leaders back home in the U.S. whom he sometimes described as "holding back" because they did not readily go along with his plans.

During our travels that summer, I concluded that M. R. was inwardly resisting the idea of retirement, which would require that he give up his work in Europe. He very graciously helped arrange for Wilbur Mullen to move to Geneva as his temporary replacement, but M. R. was so comfortable in the European setting, so personally involved in the programs he helped to initiate, that to turn everything over to someone else would be a wrenching experience.

Despite M. R.'s independent and unique way of operating, he needed an organizational base to support him—the administration "back home" that he so often criticized. For a short time, his membership on World Council of Churches committees and some other prior commitments gave him reason to return to Europe and keep in touch with various programs. But eventually these contacts diminished, which may have accounted for some of M. R.'s appearance of "lostness" in the late 1950s. The tragic loss of Amy at this time in his life also made the transition period difficult.

Several times during those weeks in 1958, I saw M. R. make blunders in dealing with Europeans, especially where matters of protocol were far more important to Europeans than they were to M. R. But in every instance, despite the embarrassment, he was always promptly forgiven by people who had learned to love him. He might not have developed a facility for using their language, as some Brethren workers did, but they responded instead to the language of his heart, which was always adequate for even the most difficult and demanding situations.

110

The Teacher and His Teachings

In an appreciative tribute to his colleague on the Bethany Seminary faculty, Dale Brown describes Floyd Mallott at work and summarizes his basic convictions.

Following a pious prayer, he might be observed shouting unreservedly, laughing heartily, whispering humorously, jumping up or down ungracefully, and pounding the desk vigorously . . . .

Some people, he would say, believe the Old Testament to be primarily oriental fairy tales. Others regard it to be matter-of-fact history. Writing these statements again, one under the other, he would then proceed to cross out "fairy tales" from the one phrase and "matter-of-fact" from the other, leaving the right description, which we would all recite in unison: "THE OLD TESTAMENT IS ORIENTAL HISTORY. . . . "

With customary Mallottian flair . . . he pontificated that when the Dunker couple first climbed into their Model T Ford and started down the highway, it was not long before the broadbrim hat flew off, then the bonnet, followed by the remainder of the distinctive attire, then many of their peculiar practices, and finally the nonresistant peace testimony. . . .

He wrote to me that nothing exhibits more effectively the genius of the Dunker church than the Love Feast-Communion service. . . . Mallott loved the ordinances of the church as embodying dialectically the two fundamentals of Christianity, the love of God and love of others . . . .

In his Apologia he stated, "For myself, I believe that the Spirit spoke at Schwarzenau, and I believe that the biblical party of the Anabaptist wing of the reformation represents in our century the clearest line of God's speaking."

The Brethren Encyclopedia. Philadelphia, Pa., and Oak Brook, Ill.: The Brethren Encyclopedia, Inc., 1983-84: 784 (sidebar).

Brown, Dale W. "Floyd Mallott: An Interpretive Essay." *Brethren Life and Thought*, Vol. XXV (1980): 97-105.

111

The Alexander Mack Seal

Important among Brethren symbols is one that bears the initials AM and obviously was originated either by Alexander Mack, a prominent leader in the beginnings of the Brethren movement, or by his son, Alexander Mack Jr., a leader among Brethren in colonial America. The original seal has not been located, but an impression showing its design and symbolism was discovered among treasures found in the old Germantown church in Pennsylvania. George N. Falkenstein, at one time a pastor of that church, tells about the discovery of the emblem and offers an interpretation of its symbolism:

> The Brethren church of Germantown has an interesting collection of old parchment deeds. While we were examining these documents from their historic interest, Mr. Julius F. Sachse discovered the impress of Mack's seal accompanying an official signature. The impression is in red sealing wax and is in perfect condition. . . . the seal consisted of several symbols, each of which had a religious significance. The entire combination constitutes a remarkable index to the character of its owner. In the center is the cross, which means sacrifice; the heart means devo-

tion, and placed on the cross, further means sacrificed in devotion; the branches of the vine mean fruit-bearing. Thus the seal reads: a devoted, fruit-bearing sacrificed life.

The seal has frequently appeared on letterheads and in publications. An example is an altar medallion in the Polo, Illinois, church, using the design of the seal. It is twelve inches in diameter and was cast in molten brass. Another is the June 7, 1958, issue of the *Gospel Messenger,* which carries an imaginary conversation between Alexander Mack and a German engraver about the formation of the seal. This dialogue, which "leans heavily upon imagination and poetic license," was written by Harry A. Brandt.

Eller, Vernard M. "Mack, Alexander, Jr." *The Brethren Encyclopedia.* Philadelphia, Pa., and Oak Brook, Ill.: The Brethren Encyclopedia, Inc., 1983-84.

Falkenstein, George N. *History of the German Baptist Brethren Church.* Lancaster, Pa., 1901.

Brandt, H. A. "The Seal Makers." *Gospel Messenger,* June 7, 1958: 6-7.

112

Mack's Personal Bible

Alexander Mack's personal Bible, now preserved in the library of Bridgewater College, had between twenty and thirty leaves of blank paper bound with it at its beginning and end. On many of these pages, Mack wrote comments that were inspired by his study of the scriptures.

This small Bible, in Luther's German translation, was printed in 1723 in Lemgo, Germany. John S. Flory, who secured it for the Bridgewater library, noted that the Bible, probably brought by Mack from Germany, was left with Alexander Mack, Jr., and then, at his death, given to the Germantown congregation, who later presented it to Philip Rothenberger, who, in turn, gave it to Henry Kurtz. Flory obtained the Bible from Kurtz's son.

Several of Mack's comments refer to God's work of creation. For example:

> It is Almighty God who created all nature, human beings as well as beasts, and when nature suffers want, God, its Creator, has mercy and comes to its assistance. . . . Oh, wonderful, eternal, and almighty Creator and Sustainer of all angels, men, and all creatures! Hallelujah!

The planet Jupiter is ninety-five times larger than the earth and is many thousands of miles in distance above the earth. Oh, what a wonderfully great and incomprehensible Creator must He be who has created and sustained such creations!

God has thus placed man in this world as in a foreign garden, in which he is to live and eat of all its fruits, but he is not allowed to take anything away with him. . . . Has it not been very wonderfully and wisely ordained by God that men have things in common such as life and body? Now Jesus says that life is more than eating and the body is more than clothing. Thus, the wealthiest people in this world have a small advantage only in the lowliest things, such as in food and clothing.

The Brethren Encyclopedia. Philadelphia, Pa., and Oak Brook, Ill.: The Brethren Encyclopedia, Inc., 1983-84: 777 (sidebar).

Durnbaugh, Donald, ed. *The Brethren in Colonial America.* Elgin, Ill.: Brethren Press, 1967.

Flory, John. S. "Alexander Mack's Bible." *Gospel Messenger*, Feb. 18, 1911: 99-100; and Feb. 25, 1911: 114.

113

The Long and the Short

A church leader can be a vigorous promoter of new ideas and still appreciate the values of a time long past. M. M. Eshelman reveals this kind of sensitivity in the early pages of his biography of "Uncle" John Metzger, which he called A Model Life. *Writing in 1898, Eshelman describes a wedding that took place around 1812 when he was a young boy.*

The people were not near so much in a hurry then, in their religious work, as some people are now. In those days they had long marriage ceremonies, preached long sermons, sang long hymns, made long prayers, and were long on everything good. Then they traveled from place to place on foot, or on ox carts, or on horse-back, and went about their work without so much rushing and hurrying. They took time to pray, to sing, to exhort. Now people are carried about by steam and electricity, on bicycles and swift horses; hence they want to be married quickly, listen to short sermons, sing short hymns fast, admire short prayers, recite short lessons, follow short methods, and, as is sometimes the case, come out with short comfort, short religion, short blessings, short life.

The Brethren Encyclopedia. Philadelphia, Pa., and Oak Brook, Ill.: The Brethren Encyclopedia, Inc., 1983-84: 455 (sidebar).
Eshelman, M. M. *A Model Life*, 1898.

George Washington Came to Dinner

—celebrity connections

114

Smarter Than They Look

The young artist viewed his assignment with some apprehension. The editor of Harper's Magazine had asked Howard Pyle to spend time among the Pennsylvania Dutch and to prepare an illustrated article. Pyle confessed in letters to his fiancée that he was at first put off by the German Baptist Brethren, but soon he learned that they were "smarter than they looked." His article and drawings, published in 1889, indicate that he came to appreciate the Brethren, whom he describes as follows:

> Here one meets the Dunker per se in every by-road and lane—men with long beards and flowing hair parted in the middle. At the farm-houses, women are pleasant, with matronly faces, stamped with humility and gentleness, while an air of almost saintly simplicity is given by the clear-starched cap, the handkerchief crossed on the breast, the white apron, and the plain gray or drab stuff of the dresses.
>
> The style of living of these good people, their manners and customs, are of the most primitive type. Their aim is to imitate the early Christians in their habits of life as well as in their religious tenets.

There is absolutely no distinction of caste among them.

. . . Their dress is of the simplest description, quaint and old-fashioned in its cut; they offer no resistance to injuries; they observe no conformity with the world and its manners and customs; they refuse to take oaths in courts of law. . . . They are called Dunkers. . . . They also sometimes call themselves "God's Peculiar People."

Howard Pyle (1835–1921) was called "the father of American illustration." He published more than three thousand illustrations in many magazines and wrote two hundred texts, many of them popular books for young readers. He was also the founder of the Brandywine School of artists and the teacher of such famous artists as N. C. Wyeth. Among his pictures of Brethren are portrayals of a love feast, drawings of an aged couple and a young couple on the way to worship, and individual pictures of sisters at worship.

The Brethren Encyclopedia. Philadelphia, Pa., and Oak Brook, Ill.: The Brethren Encyclopedia, Inc., 1983-84: 379 (sidebar).

Lehman, James H. "Howard Pyle with God's Peculiar People." *Messenger,* December 1975: 18-23.

Harper's Magazine, March 17, 1885.

Harper's New Monthly Magazine, October 1889.

115
The World Council Comes to Illinois

In 1954 the Second Assembly of the World Council of Churches met in Evanston, Illinois, just an hour away from the denominational headquarters of the Church of the Brethren. The occasion brought church leaders from around the world to the Chicago area.

One evening of the Assembly was devoted to a Chicago Symphony Orchestra concert at Ravinia Park just north of Evanston. The program included music with religious themes from symphonic or operatic numbers. Members of the Assembly, including those of us who were helpers, were given free tickets in the reserved seat section.

Just a few rows ahead of us was a section reserved for people from another denomination, but through some mistake on the part of the ushers, the seats were taken by people from another group.

One of our group, W. Harold Row, immediately noticed the mixup when the bishop of the group discovered that the reserved seats for his people were already taken. Row commented to us, "Now you'll see the bishop pull rank." The bishop, using his authority as the leader of a large denomination, declared that these seats were provided for him, not the strangers who came in first.

The ushers were embarrassed, but the people who were there by mistake offered to leave. They were impressed with the bishop's rotundity which seemed to underscore his profundity. Though the incident was resolved without difficulty, observers were impressed by the churchman's reliance on his rank to get special attention.

Later, Harold Row told us that when he made a plea for more aid at one of the World Council committee meetings, the bishop who had pulled rank, after some initial reluctance, asked his denomination to make a larger gift for the aid of refugees.

J. Henry Long, who was serving as an audio-visual consultant for the Church of the Brethren, and I received an invitation to attend an informal reception for the five presidents of the World Council. One of the dignitaries was Geoffrey Fisher, the Archbishop of Canterbury, who had crowned Queen Elizabeth II.

It was apparent that the World Council leaders were thoroughly exhausted from meeting so many people.

As I was quickly trying to decide how I should appropriately address the archbishop, Henry, who was ahead of me in line, surprised and shocked me when he so informally greeted the archbishop, saying, "Well, it looks as though you have had a long, hard day." The archbishop, who was quite short, gave a great sigh and placed his hands on Henry's broad shoulders and completely relaxed against him. That was all that was needed, no salutation, no protocol, no other comment.

After a moment or so, Geoffrey Fisher smiled directly and understandingly at Henry. The archbishop seemed grateful for the simplicity of that brief interval.

116

Diplomacy Brethren-Style

In 1977, when Andrew Young was serving as U.S. ambassador to the United Nations, he told the Church of the Brethren Annual Conference at Richmond, Virginia, that "my first diplomatic experience was the six weeks I spent in a Brethren work camp in Austria with representatives of some twenty different nations, and the travels through Europe with Brethren Volunteer Service in the early 1950s. In this I discerned that diplomacy was not just a matter of principles and treaties and ideals, but essentially a people-to-people phenomenon."

Young also recalled attending a youth meeting at Camp Mack that encouraged him to begin "the pursuit of a more non-violent way of life."

Young's wife, the former Jean Childs, graduated from Manchester College in 1954.

The Brethren Encyclopedia. Philadelphia, Pa., and Oak Brook, Ill.: The Brethren Encyclopedia, Inc., 1983-84: 1367 (sidebar).

Young, Andrew. "An Agenda for Brethren." *Messenger*, October 1977: 16-19.

117

Peace

An unassuming circle of salt-and-pepper granite stones, located in a nature preserve and bird sanctuary just a fifteen-minute walk from the Juniata College campus in Huntingdon, Pennsylvania, was designed for group meditation by a young Chinese woman, Maya Lin. A piece of round polished granite created for private meditation is set in the trees on an adjoining hill.

The vision for this non-denominational open-air peace chapel at Juniata was that of Elizabeth Evans Baker, who commissioned its design and construction in 1988. The architect, Maya Lin, had already won international recognition for her creation in the simplicity and artistry of the Vietnam Veterans Memorial in Washington, D.C., which draws visitors from around the world and causes them to reflect on the personal devastation of war.

In October of 1989, Maya Lin returned to the campus for the dedication of the Baker Peace Chapel. She is also featured in an Academy Award-winning 1995 documentary, "Maya Lin: A Strong Clear Vision," which includes scenes of the chapel and her personal account of the decade of work and political process by which she sees and develops her unusual structures. She says, "The audience is very much a part of my artwork—wherein the work does not become complete until the viewer experiences it—giving him or her a sense of responsibility."

"Open-air Worship." *Messenger*, August/September 1990: 5.

118

No Such Thing as Fear

At age ten Chester Melvin Vaniman, who was generally known as Melvin, watched a balloon flight near his farm home in central Illinois and began to dream of seeing the world. The year was 1876. He was later to visit many countries and help design dirigibles capable of transoceanic travel, but not until he had attended Mt. Morris College (Academy), sung in the chorus of a traveling light opera company, projected what may have been the first motion pictures seen in San Francisco, and built a camera said to have contained the largest photographic lens known at the time. He also set his sights on being part of the first expedition to reach the North Pole.

Until 1904 Vaniman maintained steady contact by letter with his relatives in the Pleasant Hill (Illinois) congregation, where his uncle Daniel was a prominent Brethren leader.

In Paris in 1904, Melvin Vaniman helped Walter Wellman construct a new "rigid balloon," or dirigible, for an attempt to reach the North Pole, but Admiral Peary got there first. In a subsequent effort to cross the Atlantic Ocean in a dirigible, Vaniman and other crew members had to abandon their craft at sea, but were rescued. Then, in 1911 and 1912, Melvin Vaniman and his brother Calvin worked on the dirigible *Akron* in preparation for another transatlantic crossing. They were killed instantly when the aircraft exploded on a test flight near Atlantic City, New Jersey. An obituary in the *Mt. Morris Index* in September 1912 said of Melvin, "He loved adventure and knew no such thing as fear."

The Brethren Encyclopedia. Philadelphia, Pa., and Oak Brook, Ill.: The Brethren Encyclopedia, Inc., 1983-84: 1303 (sidebar).
Weddle, Edith Harshbarger. *Pleasant Hill.* Elgin, Ill.: Brethren Press, 1956.

119

Nobel Prize Winner in Atomic Research

Harold C. Urey (1893–1981), who won the Nobel Prize for chemistry in 1934 after he discovered deuterium or heavy hydrogen, was the son of Samuel Clayton and Clara Reinoehl Urey. His father, a schoolteacher and Brethren minister in Walkerton, Indiana, died when Harold was six years old.

Urey was clerk of the Cedar Lake, Indiana, congregation as a young man. He left Indiana for studies that took him to universities in Montana and California and eventually to the Niels Bohr Institute in Copenhagen, Denmark. Later he taught at leading universities in the United States and Britain and developed a widely accepted theory of the gaseous origins of planets.

Although Urey's discovery of the deuterium isotope aided the development of the atomic bomb and although he was at one time head of atomic bomb research at Columbia University, he later actively opposed nuclear weapons. He warned that "atomic bombs are evil. . . . and cannot be used to maintain peace." His small book *I Am a Frightened Man* had wide distribution.

The Brethren Encyclopedia. Philadelphia, Pa., and Oak Brook, Ill.: The Brethren Encyclopedia, Inc., 1983-84: 1298 (sidebar).

120
Candidate for Sainthood

The daughter of a Brethren woman who married into the wealthy Drexel family of Philadelphia became one of the country's most generous supporters of schools for African Americans and American Indians. She was Sister Mary Katharine Drexel (1858–1955), founder of the Order of the Sisters of the Blessed Sacrament. Giving up her social position as a member of a prominent family, she followed a religious vocation at the age of thirty, choosing for many years to live on less than a dollar a day while she poured more than a thousand dollars a day into the charitable and educational projects she initiated and supported. Over a period of sixty-four years, she contributed to other causes an estimated $17,500,000 from her inheritance.

Katharine Drexel was the daughter of Francis A. Drexel, a banker and partner of J. P. Morgan. Her mother, Hannah Jane Langstroth, was baptized by the German Baptist Brethren in 1850. Hannah died just thirty-four days after Katharine was born, leaving her two young daughters motherless. She was buried in the Germantown Brethren cemetery, but in 1946 her body was moved to the burial chapel of the Drexel family.

Katharine Drexel traveled widely in order to know personally the conditions of American Indians in the west and African Americans in the south. Her contributions helped to establish Xavier University (New Orleans), an institution aiding the education of blacks. It was with her in mind that an act of Congress in 1921 amended the income tax law to free from tax the income of people who gave ninety percent or more of their income to charity.

Although Katharine Drexel never knew her Brethren mother and was devoted to her stepmother, according to one biographer, she and her sister, Elizabeth, regularly visited the Langstroth home in Germantown where they played with their cousins and learned to crochet from their grandmother, who wore the Brethren plain dress.

Katharine Drexel was often called "saintly." An official petition that she be regarded as a saint by the Roman Catholic Church was introduced in 1964 by Cardinal John Krol of Philadelphia. The procedure leading toward canonization was advanced in 1977 by the appointment of a church official to further her cause. According to the *Chicago Tribune*, in 1988 Pope John Paul II beatified her after the Vatican approved a miracle that was attributed to her intercession. To eventually become a saint, the Vatican will have to confirm a second such miracle attributed to her. If the canonization of Mother Katherine comes about, she will be the first official "saint" with a Brethren mother.

The Brethren Encyclopedia. Philadelphia, Pa., and Oak Brook, Ill.: The Brethren Encyclopedia, Inc., 1983-84: 405 (sidebar).
Burton, Katherine, *The Golden Door: The Life of Katherine Drexel,* New York, P. J. Kennedy and Sons, 1957.
Howe, Roland. *The History of a Church.* Philadelphia, 1943.
Chicago Tribune, Nov. 21, 1988.

121

Famous American Sculptor

An American sculptor who grew up in a Brethren farm home near Union Bridge, Maryland, completed the models for two sets of bronze doors in the U. S. Capitol. He also sculpted the statue of Chief Justice Roger B. Taney that stands in front of the Maryland State House.

He was William H. Rinehart (1825–1874), the son of Israel and Mary Snader Rinehart. As a youth, William worked in marble quarries near Union Bridge and on his father's farm. Later he became an apprentice stonecutter in Baltimore. He studied sculpture in Florence, Italy, from 1855 to 1857. From 1858 until his death in 1874 he lived in Rome, Italy, except for brief visits to Maryland.

The original designs for the bronze doors of the U.S. Capitol building were made by Thomas Crawford. After Crawford's death Rinehart was commissioned to execute the models used for casting doors. He shipped the models for the Senate doors (on the east portico entrance) from Italy in 1864 and models for the House of Representatives doors (on the east portico entrance) in 1867. In each set of doors, there are scenes from American history, equally divided between acts of war and deeds of peace.

William Rinehart also fashioned a clay bust of his mother, Mary Snader Rinehart, wearing the bonnet common among the Dunkers.

The Brethren Encyclopedia. Philadelphia, Pa., and Oak Brook, Ill.: The Brethren Encyclopedia, Inc., 1983-84: 1110 (sidebar).

Scharf, A. M. *History of Western Maryland*, Vol. II. Philadelphia: Louis H. Everts, 1882.

Ankrum, Freeman. *Maryland and Pennsylvania Historical Sketches*. Masontown, Pa.: n.p., 1947.

122

Actor in Action for Peace

It was no surprise that Don Murray, born in Hollywood in 1929, should choose a career as an actor. What was unusual was his decision at age eighteen to be a conscientious objector. A few years later this choice took him to New Windsor, Maryland, and to alternative service overseas at Kassel, Germany (where Don was baptized in the Fulda River), and to Naples, Italy, where he worked with refugees who were unable to find resettlement opportunities. Back home in 1955, Murray soon won national recognition for his acting, but his determination to help the homeless was reflected in the financial support and publicity he was able to solicit for a program he founded called HELP (Homeless European Land Program), which helped to resettle World War II refugees on the island of Sardinia (Italy).

Murray also insisted on acting roles that would support his religious and humanitarian convictions. Toward this end he helped to write, direct, and produce, as well as act, in films that would meet his standards, such as *The Hoodlum Priest* (*Time* magazine said of one scene: "A new dimension of reality surrounds and penetrates the scene: the dimension of divine love"), *The Confessions of Tom Harris* (the story of a rapist who was transformed into a man of love), and *The Homeless* (a television program illustrating the plight of 45,000 refugees in western Europe).

Concerning his association with the Church of the Brethren, Murray wrote in 1958, "I found there were ways I could serve my country other than by fighting. I volunteered with the Church of the Brethren for overseas duty. In their training sessions, the Brethren impressed me tremendously as people who freely give a portion of their lives to make themselves useful to others. . . . I made a commitment to try to lead my life that way."

The Brethren Encyclopedia. Philadelphia, Pa., and Oak Brook, Ill.: The Brethren Encyclopedia, Inc., 1983-84: 625-26 (sidebar).
Brethren Historical Library and Archives, biography files, Elgin, Ill.

123

Vixen or Devotee?

When John Greenleaf Whittier was writing *Snow-Bound*, his popular poem about his boyhood home, he could not have known then in 1866 that the "not-unfeared, half-welcome guest" to whom he devoted eighty lines would soon be laid to rest in an unmarked grave in the Brethren cemetery at Germantown.

She was Harriet Livermore, a strange figure who visited many eastern communities as a preacher and a pilgrim, though she was not always welcome in churches. One exception was the Crown Street church in Philadelphia where she communed with the Brethren in 1826 and where Sarah Righter Major, whom she called "my daughter," was baptized as a result of her preaching.

Harriet Livermore was a frequent visitor in the Whittier home, including the occasion when the family was snow-bound. The poet saw her as a brilliant and gifted person whose "cultured phrase" rebuked "our homeliness of words and ways." He later described her complex nature:

> A woman tropical, intense
> In thought and act, in soul and sense,

She blended in a like degree
The vixen and the devotee
Revealing with each freak or feint
The temper of Petruchio's Kate,
The raptures of Siena's saint.

For the pilgrim-stranger, Whittier felt compassion:

Where'er her troubled path may be,
The Lord's sweet pity with her go!
The outward, wayward life we see,
The hiddensprings we may not know.

Some people who knew Harriet Livermore thought Whittier dealt too harshly with her. Abraham Harley Cassel, who collected all her writings and papers and who assisted her biographer, S. T. Livermore, in his research for *The Pilgrim Stranger* (1884), observed that "she had all the faults that Whittier speaks of, but while he appears to have been so well acquainted with her, he must certainly have known her virtues as well as her faults."

In later editions of *Snow-Bound*, Whittier added a preface to his poem in which he summarized Harriet Livermore's unusual career. He called her "a young woman of fine natural ability, enthusiastic, eccentric . . .

equally ready to exhort in schoolhouse prayer meetings and dance in the Washington ballroom, while her father was a member of Congress."

The Brethren Encyclopedia. Philadelphia, Pa., and Oak Brook, Ill.: The Brethren Encyclopedia, Inc., 1983-84: 750-51 (sidebar).

Whittier, John Greenleaf. *Complete Poetical Works*. Houghton Mifflin Company, 1908.

Long, Harvey L. "Harriet Livermore, Guest of the Brethren." *Brethren Life and Thought*, Vol. XXIV (1979): 220-224.

Ankrum, Freeman. "The Pilgrim Stranger." *Gospel Messenger*, Nov. 25, 1950: 10-11.

124

A Secret Baptism?

Although there is no documented evidence that Abraham Lincoln was ever a member of any church, he has been claimed by many religious groups—including the Brethren. Presbyterians note that he attended Presbyterian churches, of which his wife was a member, in Springfield and Washington. Some of Lincoln's ancestors were Quakers. As a boy he attended a Baptist church. There are claims that he was a Swedenborgian, a spiritualist, a believer in universal salvation. A minister of the Christian Church was reported to have baptized Lincoln secretly in a creek near Springfield shortly before his inauguration as president of the United States.

This story is similar to one circulated by some Brethren who declared that Isaac Billheimer of Rossville or Heath, Indiana, either baptized Lincoln or was acquainted with the minister who did. This version claims that Lincoln met the minister one night near Springfield and that, after the baptism in a river, the minister returned home by train, the president promising that he would conform to the order of the church after completing his term of office. Another version of the Brethren baptism identifies a time of crisis in Lincoln's life in 1862 when, following a breakdown, he was said to have asked D. P. Sayler to baptize him in the Potomac River. Yet another anecdote tells of Lincoln's baptism by Elder George Wolfe.

A more plausible Lincoln story, often repeated among Brethren, describes one of the many visits of D. P. Sayler, a Maryland elder, to the White House. On this occasion the president was reported to have said, "Brother Sayler, I ordain you a Dunker preacher forever."

The Brethren Encyclopedia. Philadelphia, Pa., and Oak Brook, Ill.: The Brethren Encyclopedia, Inc., 1983-84: 743 (sidebar).

125

The Companionship, the Acceptance

Nathan Leopold (1904–1971) was sentenced to life imprisonment in 1924 for the murder of a boy he and Richard Loeb had kidnaped; he was paroled from Stateville Prison (Joliet, Illinois) in 1958. On many occasions he expressed his appreciation for the willingness of the Brethren Service Commission to accept him upon his parole as a medical technician at its hospital in Puerto Rico. He wrote in an article for *Brethren Life and Thought*, "So far as I am aware, mine was the first case in which the Brethren sponsored a man released from prison on parole. To me the Brethren Service Commission offered the job, the home, and the sponsorship without which a man cannot be paroled. But it gave me so much more than that, the companionship, the acceptance, the love which would have rendered a violation of parole almost impossible."

Leopold especially cherished the friendship of W. Harold Row, executive secretary of the Brethren Service Commission, who accompanied him when he left prison for service in Puerto Rico. He said, "I was privileged to know Harold for over thirteen years; I saw him at least once a year and generally more. And each time

I could spend time with him, it was as if I were morally refreshed and reinvigorated."

The Brethren Encyclopedia. Philadelphia, Pa., and Oak Brook, Ill.: The Brethren Encyclopedia, Inc., 1983-84: 738 (sidebar).

Leopold, Nathan. *Life Plus 99 Years.* Westport, Conn.: Greenwood Press, 1974.

Leopold, Nathan. "The Ministry of the Brethren in the Years to Come." *Brethren Life and Thought*, Vol. X (1965): 4-12.

126

"My Resurrected Voice"

The autobiography of world-renowned actor James Earl Jones is dedicated first to his "natural father," Robert Earl Jones, who also was a talented actor. But there is another dedication—to Donald E. Crouch, whom Jones identifies as the "father of my resurrected voice." Jones's book, *Voices and Silences*, records a remarkable life in which he has achieved new successes almost every year in television and in the theater, including spectacular performances in the plays *Othello* and *The Great White Hope*. His rich, deep voice has often been described as a powerful gift; he himself has said that he grew up with the "spoken word."

James Earl Jones was born in Mississippi where he lived with his grandparents who uprooted the family and moved to a farm in Michigan when he was just starting elementary school. For whatever reason, the move was very traumatic and caused the young Jones to stutter so much that he spent the next several years nearly mute, almost losing the power of speech. He says of that period in his life, "When I entered high school, I had gotten through eight years of school without using the power of speech, unless I was forced to."

Jones attended high school in Brethren, Michigan. It was a small building with a few rooms for both junior high and high school classes. Donald E. Crouch, a former high school and college English teacher and a member of the Church of the Brethren, came out of retirement to teach English in that school in Brethren. As a "man of poetry," Professor Crouch introduced the afflicted boy to good literature—Shakespeare, Emerson, Longfellow. The young high school student became so inspired that he began to write poetry that impressed Crouch very much. At Crouch's urging, the mute boy was challenged to read his poetry aloud to the class. Astonishingly, the words flowed smoothly and Jones was on his way to "recapturing [his] ability to speak." From that point on, Jones honed his public speaking and interpretive reading skills, going on to win the championship award for public speaking from his high school and a scholarship to the University of Michigan.

Jones continued to read Emerson, following the good advice of Professor Crouch: "If you read enough Emerson, when you go into your adult life and choose your career, no matter what you do, you will do it well."

Apparently James Earl Jones read enough Emerson that he has been able to do many things well in his adult life—including 250 productions since 1950, one of the most recent being the leading role of Stephen Kumalo in Alan Paton's memorable *Cry, the Beloved Country*, a story with poetic and haunting descriptions of South Africa that seem to call for a voice that is deep and "resurrected."

Professor Donald Crouch was a Church of the Brethren minister whose family, on coming to Michigan from New England, became active in the Church of the Brethren in Brethren. Brethren, Michigan, the only town in the U.S. named for the church, according to historian Don Stroup, got its start in 1902, when a land swindler lured German Baptist Brethren to the area with the promise of cheap land, fertile soil, and a long growing season. As an added attraction, the developer even named the town "Brethren." Upon their arrival, however, the Brethren discovered why the land was cheap. It wasn't fertile and the growing season was short. But many settlers were forced to tough it out, having burned their bridges behind them.

Jones, James Earl and Penelope Niven. *Voices and Silences*. New York: Charles Scribner's Sons, Macmillan Pub. Co., 1993.

127

George Washington Came to Dinner

Christian Ebersole was a Brethren farmer in Washington County, Maryland, who hosted George Washington and a group of aides when they were looking for a site for the future capital of the United States. Ebersole's daughter, who died in 1859 at the age of 92, shared her memories of the event with her children, specifically Jacob Forrer, who passed them on to James Quinter, editor of The Primitive Christian and Pilgrim. *This is Quinter's account:*

[Jacob Forrer's mother] remembered very distinctly General Washington and his appearance. . . . When he and a number of the men of note of his time were selecting a site for the Capital of the United States, they visited the country about Hagerstown, as that place was thought of as the site of the seat of Government. The persons in the company, whose business it was to provide for the entertainment of the company, called at the house of Mr. Ebersole and desired to make preparations there for General Washington and his suite to dine. Mr. Ebersole modestly suggested some other place, that of a more distinguished man. . . . But General Washington had heard something of Mr. Ebersole and desired to make his house his stopping-place. . . .

The General's company had its cooks and many of the conveniences needed for the preparation of the dinner. There were some things, however, they desired the family to furnish, and these were at once supplied. Sister Forrer remembered the manner in which the company partook of the dinner, or the way in which they conducted themselves at the table. When they were seated, some thirty or more in number, General Washington said grace, and there was no levity at the table. . . . When the company was about leaving, the proper person asked for the bill, but he was told that the honor of entertaining such a company was a sufficient compensation. He, however, took out a ten dollar gold piece, and when it was refused, it was thrown down with the remark, "Give it to the girls."

The Brethren Encyclopedia. Philadelphia, Pa., and Oak Brook, Ill.: The Brethren Encyclopedia, Inc., 1983-84: 1320 (sidebar).

"Our Visit to Virginia."*The Primitive Christian and Pilgrim*, May 28, 1878.

128

A Singular Instance in the History of Mankind

Benjamin Franklin was impressed with the reluctance of Brethren to print a confession of faith that would be binding on all members. In his Autobiography *he records a conversation with Michael Welfare (Wohlfahrt), whom he mistakenly identifies as one of the founders of the Brethren. (Wohlfahrt was indeed baptized by the Brethren in 1725, but he later became a leader of the Ephrata community.) Franklin writes:*

[Welfare] complained to me that [the Dunkers] were grievously calumniated by the zealots of other persuasions, and charged with abominable principles and practices to which they were utter strangers. I told him this had always been the case with new sects, and that to put a stop to such abuse I imagined it might be well to publish the articles of their belief and the rules of their discipline. He said that it had been proposed among them, but not agreed to, for this reason: "When we were first drawn together as a society," says he, "it had pleased God to enlighten our minds so far as to see that some doctrines, which we had once esteemed truths were errors; and that others, which we esteemed errors, were real truths. From time to time He has been pleased to afford us farther light, and our principles have been improving, and errors diminishing. Now we are not sure that we are arrived at the end of this progression, and at the perfection of spiritual or theological knowledge; and we fear that, if we should print our confession, we should feel ourselves as if bound and confined by it, and perhaps be unwilling to receive farther improvement, and our successors still more so, as conceiving what we their elders and founders had done, to be something sacred, never to be departed from."

This modesty in a sect is perhaps a singular instance in the history of mankind, every other sect supposing itself in possession of all truth, and that those who differ are so far in the wrong.

The Brethren Encyclopedia. Philadelphia, Pa., and Oak Brook, Ill.: The Brethren Encyclopedia, Inc., 1983-84: 943 (sidebar).

Franklin, Benjamin. *Autobiography.* New York: Henry Holt and Co., 1912.

129

Witness to an Assassination

More than sixty years after it happened, Emma Nice Ellis could describe vividly an incident she observed in 1901—the assassination of the president of the United States. As a young woman she was visiting the Pan-American Exposition in Buffalo, New York. On September 6, 1901, she attended a public reception for President William McKinley in the Temple of Music, where she took her place among hundreds of people waiting in line to shake hands with the chief executive. There were only a few people ahead of her when she noticed a man, later identified as an anarchist named Leon Czolgosz, whose arm was wrapped in a bandage. Suddenly a shot rang out—from a revolver hidden in the bandaged hand. The president was rushed to a hospital where he died several days later. The assassin was taken into custody, and Emma Ellis was among the people questioned for firsthand reports of the shooting, which she described as an "awful experience."

The Brethren Encyclopedia. Philadelphia, Pa., and Oak Brook, Ill.: The Brethren Encyclopedia, Inc., 1983-84: 442 (sidebar).
Recorded interview, Brethren Historical Library and Archives, Elgin, Ill.

130

Little Miss Sureshot

The woman who received worldwide acclaim for her sharpshooting, who traveled for seventeen years with Buffalo Bill's Wild West Show, whose stage name was Annie Oakley but whom Chief Sitting Bull called "Little Miss Sureshot," grew up in Darke County, Ohio, where Brethren were among her friends and neighbors.

When Annie was six years old (she lived from 1860 to 1926), her father died and her mother married a neighbor, Daniel Brumbaugh, an elderly man who lived only a few years more before he too passed away. Many years later Annie Oakley claimed Martin Grove Brumbaugh as a cousin, and frequently she and her husband Frank Butler (whom she defeated in a shooting match before she married him at age sixteen) visited the Brethren educator at his home in Germantown, Pennsylvania.

Her biographers and the people who knew Annie Oakley describe her as "modest," "soft-spoken," "surprisingly feminine," "quiet and sedate," and even "puritanical" in her private life, not at all like the heroine of the musical *Annie Get Your Gun.* Seriously injured in an auto accident in 1921, Annie Oakley and her husband returned to Greeneville, Ohio. Her niece reported that she heard her pray, just before her death in 1926, "Oh that I might live over again those days of simplicity, when God was consulted and asked to guide the little family through each day."

The Brethren Encyclopedia. Philadelphia, Pa., and Oak Brook, Ill.: The Brethren Encyclopedia, Inc., 1983-84: 958 (sidebar).

Swartwout, Annie Fern. *Missie, An Historical Biography of Annie Oakley.* Blanchester, Ohio: Brown Pub. Co., 1947.

Havighurst, Walter. *Annie Oakley of the Wild West.* Lincoln, Neb.: Bison Books (University of Nebraska Press), 1954, 1992.

According to the Studebaker family history (*The Studebaker Family in America, 1736–1976*), Annie Oakley went to live at age eight with David and Mary Jane Studebaker near Greeneville, Ohio. They were likely Methodist rather than Brethren. This is not mentioned in the biography written by Annie's niece (Swartwout), although the niece records that at that age Annie went to work for a family who treated her badly and whom Annie refused to identify by their real names.

Annie Oakley may have had more than a Brethren connection in her mother's family, who lived near Hollidaysburg, Pennsylvania. Annie's grandmother was a

Clapper, the daughter of one of the early Brethren Clapper families living near Hollidaysburg. The biographer, also of the same family, refers to Annie's parents as having been Quaker. To my knowledge, there were no Quaker meetings in that part of Pennsylvania but, of course, many Brethren. The Clapper history devotes a page to Annie Oakley's family but does not claim to have written records to prove the connection. K. M.

Index

About the author

Kenneth I. Morse is retired editor of *Messenger* magazine for the Church of the Brethren. He is also former book editor and editor of youth publications for the Church of the Brethren General Board. In his retirement, Morse has served as a writer and member of the editorial staff and Board of Editors for *The Brethren Encyclopedia*. The author of numerous hymns and poems, Ken Morse is perhaps best known for the popular hymn "Move in our midst." He was a member of the hymnal committees for both *The Brethren Hymnal* (1951) and *Hymnal: A Worship Book* (1992). He and his wife, Marjorie, live in North Manchester, Indiana.